What people are saying...

"This makes it so easy to build your vocabulary through reading! I majored in English and as a word lover myself, I recognized many of the words in this book but still found myself looking at the definitions that were provided just to be sure I understood their meaning. Especially with all of the dumbed-down and questionable literature being published for young adults these days, such a series has tremendous potential to actually enhance their knowledge while upholding positive moral values."

—Teri Ann Berg Olsen, *Knowledge House*

"Burk's style is easy for the reader and geared to teenagers in the high school years. This book has 300 words that, for the most part, will be new to the reader... What an incredible way to increase the writing and speaking skills of your student!"

—Jennifer Barker, *The Old Schoolhouse Magazine*

"There are very few better ways to quickly read and actually remember 300 high-level words, such as "ruminate," "lachrymose," "salubrious" and "pulchritude." Some of the words may be recognized by many readers, but even this reader was learning new words throughout."

—Chloe O'Connor, *The Signal*

"Besides being an excellent tool to enhance vocabulary and language development, pre-teens and teens will find the story engaging. Best of all, the story steers clear of offensive language and unsavory themes."

—Anne Gebhart, *Heart of Texas*

D0167779

Books in VocabCafé Series

PLANET EXILE

By Josh Burk

Vocab
Café

Maven of Memory Publishing
Hurst, Texas

Planet Exile

ISBN 978-0-9833277-0-7

The VocabCafé Book Series is intended to encourage the study and investigation of the English language. This book is not, nor does it purport itself to be, the complete and final authority on word usage and definitions. Maven of Memory Publishing is not responsible for any errors, omissions, or misunderstandings contained in this book or derived from information contained herein.

Cover and layout by impact studios

Printed in the United States of America

To Mom and Dad,

Thank you for always supporting me and my endeavors.
If my life has any meaning at all, it's because of your
benevolence.

An Introduction to VocabCafé

The purpose of the VocabCafé book series is to encourage the development of vocabulary knowledge. At Maven of Memory Publishing we believe that a good understanding of vocabulary words is crucial to lifelong success. Contained inside this novella are more than 300 words that can be helpful in improving the vocabulary of any reader, which can lead to better reading, writing, and speaking skills. It can also help improve test scores for students intending to take standardized exams.

Every vocabulary word is placed in the context of a narrative story. The storyline and sentences surrounding the words should help readers easily deduce their meanings. For easy reference and instant reinforcement, the literal definitions of every word are at the bottom of each page. At the end of each chapter there is a review of the vocabulary words featured in that section. We recommend that you go over this word review immediately after finishing the chapter in order to study the definitions while their context remains fresh.

These books were written with an intended audience of high school teenagers, although many parents find them appropriate for younger students. As a family-based company, our goal is to make a quality product that can be enjoyed by everyone. These stories contain no magic, sorcery, swear words, or illicit situations. Nonetheless, we recommend that parents read every book (not just ours) that they give their children to make sure the messages and themes coincide with their beliefs and standards.

Accompanying flash cards organized by chapter are available for purchase and highly recommended to help ensure success. Each card has the word definition and its use in the story. Reviewing these will help you in your quest for mastery of vocabulary words.

We hope this series is instrumental in helping you advance your proficiency with the English language.

Good Luck!
The VocabCafé Team

PLANET EXILE

1

Thump... Thump... Thump...

Maleck's heartbeat echoed through his ears. He panted anxiously.

Did they see me? he worried.

Shivering with cold in the dark alleyway, Maleck stood *aplomb,* leaning against the cool cement wall, wishing he could turn invisible. If only he felt confident and *aplomb,* but at this moment he was overwhelmed by a deep uncertainty.

Where's Jemini?

Footsteps clamored along the road, with the unmistakable cadence of U-zone soldiers. One-two-three. One-two-three. The cadence proved that hiding wasn't an option. There was no turning back now.

Maleck pulled his hood further down his brow and continued to walk. The *glacial* wind icily pierced his young hands as he moved. *Why did his parents move him to Acritas?* All his problems stemmed from that, at least in Maleck's opinion. They thought the urban landscape would help their lonely child socialize, but in reality the transition only served to further *disaffect* him from his peers. He did make

---

Aplomb	(uh-**plom**) – N – (1)vertical position; (2)having poise
Glacial	(**gley**-shuhl) – ADJ – bitterly cold; moving slowly
Disaffect	(dis-uh-**fekt**) – V – to alienate the affections

one friend though—Jemini, whose safety was the whole reason for this excursion.

His feet stepped faster and faster, not out of fear, but rather by an instinctual desire to escape the elements. He'd be at his destination in only a few blocks. He could do his business, then go.

He could hear chatter coming from behind at a distance. This sparked Maleck's first moment of actual panic. He couldn't get caught. The streets had a reputation for mischievous vagrants, so his *interloping* was a crime not easily overlooked.

The dumpster standing ahead, although not the *paragon* of perfect hiding places, would have to do. Besides, Maleck had never been afraid to immerse himself in the refuse of everyday life. He kind of liked being dirty, which was apparent by his constantly disheveled appearance. His wavy black hair hadn't seen a razor since his 13th birthday, and he was clearly on his way to 16 and a half at this juncture. He liked the mystery of long hair, and the way it seemed to hide him from the stares of onlookers.

Hands first, he plowed into the trash, his left sleeve immediately soaking up something slimy and wet. This intensified the feeling of cold throughout Maleck's body. He tried to breathe silently through his nose, but the horrific smell still hit him full force.

I just have to wait until the guards pass.

The marching continued outside, moving closer and closer. When the soldiers reached the trash can, they stopped.

It's over. He thought. *They know.*

Interlope	(**in**-ter-lohp) – V – to intrude without approval
Paragon	(**par**-uh-gon) – N – model of excellence

A gruff voice belted a few incoherent orders, and then the group of men ran off excitedly. Their footsteps began to trail away. Maleck waited until he was sure they were gone. When no more sounds could be heard, he exited his hiding place.

He had made it. The Orin Bauchman Foundation was a large futuristic academy that stood ominously among the crammed structures in the center of Acritas. The OBF, or Overbearing Brainwash Facility, was the moniker Maleck had lovingly bestowed upon this place that had become his school. The name never caught on with the other students.

The plan was simple: jump over the fence, climb the stairs, and tag the front entryway. No one had ever **defiled** the immaculate entrance of the OBF before, so this stunt would be remembered for years to come. The **notoriety** was definitely appealing for someone who rarely got attention from his peers.

Two other motivating factors prompted Maleck's action. First was the influence of his acquaintance, Jemini. If tracks existed in Acritas, this boy would be from the wrong side of them. Fortunately for him, travel by train had been abolished 300 years ago. Jemini was a loner, a goof-off, and a general mischief-maker. Maleck liked him.

The idea was hatched during lunch as a kind of test to see if Maleck had what it took to be his friend. Maleck knew that if he could pull off this initiation task, he might actually find a true **crony** in Jemini. They were supposed to meet at 10 PM and complete the prank together, but

Defile	(dih-**fahyl**) – V – to make impure or dirty
Notoriety	(noh-tuh-**rahy**-i-tee) – N – state of being known widely, esp. unfavorably
Crony	(**kroh**-nee) – N – a close friend; chum

Jemini hadn't shown up. It was well past midnight before Maleck decided to head out alone. He couldn't resist the thought of using his XPS.

The Xandcorp Professional Stylex was released publicly in October. Maleck got a bootleg version in June. Capable of producing a 7-kilowatt beam, the XPS could etch inscriptions on stone surfaces within a matter of seconds; and being the size of a writing pen, it was the perfect tool for illegal graffiti. For Maleck, it had an obvious appeal: the ability to forever carve his name in the wall by laser. The graffiti artistry of the typical city *gamin* had advanced since the age of spray paint.

As Maleck bounded over the fence, he experienced overwhelming satisfaction. His ***brazen*** attempt at greatness made him excited to be alive. At this moment he felt no fear. Nothing could stop him now.

He climbed the marble stairs to the front of the OBF, and pulled out his XPS.

–ICONOCLAST– he seared rebelliously into the white wall. Maleck had embraced the word ever since learning its definition. He was a young rebel standing in the face of conformity and daring to take on the large conglomeration of collective conscience and speak as an individual without fear. That is, until he heard the sirens.

In a flash, Maleck found himself surrounded by red lights. All those marching U-zone soldiers appeared around him. He turned timidly from his art to face what felt like a firing squad.

Gamin	(**gam**-in) – N – street urchin
Brazen	(**brey**-zuhn) – ADJ – shameless or impudent; like brass
Iconoclast	(ahy-**kon**-uh-klast) – N – a person who attacks cherished beliefs

Out stepped E6, a muscle-bound monster with a fear-inducing presence. His voice pounded through the air like thunder:

"Maleck Vise Plutean, you're under arrest."

Instinctively, Maleck knew something was off. *How did the officer know his name?* He raised his hands in surrender.

"I give up. You got me."

* * *

At least the holding tank is warm, Maleck thought as he sat alone in a freshly laundered jumpsuit. He'd been in trouble before; he'd get out of it again. After all, his parents were part of the high council. They would probably be horrifically angry, but at least he'd earn the respectful *paean* of Jemini, who was too chicken to try the stunt himself.

That's when he entered. *Jemini?*

"How's it going, Maleck?"

"They caught you, too?" he responded.

"No, I may have **belied** my connection with the cops; this whole thing was a setup."

"What do you mean?"

"I mean a few months back, I got caught stealing some Zoom Shoes. As part of my probation I was asked to narc on others kids. I'm sorry. I've got two more months of service left, and I wanted to make sure you kept my involvement in this whole thing a secret… So I can continue to spy."

Maleck was dumbfounded, unable to respond. His new friend, his only hope of someone to talk to, was

---

Paean	(**pee**-uhn) – N – any song of praise or joy
Belie	(bih-**lahy**) – V – to show to be false; to misrepresent

a complete *charlatan*, misrepresenting himself the whole time.

I can't believe I fell for this!

"If it's any consolation, I don't think you're going to get into too much trouble. Your parents have pretty much taken care of everything," Jemini added.

"Thank you; it's not any consolation."

Jemini nodded knowingly. "I'd be pretty sore about it, too."

He left Maleck alone in the empty cell with his thoughts swirling around in his brain. *What's going to happen now?* Maleck knew his parents were more than fed up with his behavior. He knew his punishment would be *imponderably* severe, so bad he couldn't even conceive of it. His fears were confirmed by the arrival of Azreel and Beol Vise Plutean. Husband and wife, they appeared the perfect complement to one another. Both wearing spotless white uniforms, they had the presence of royalty and an air of distinction.

Beol, Maleck's *Junoesque* mother, leaned down to her son and took his hands. She had a weathered face and slightly graying hair, but a warm and kind smile.

"Why must you show such bitter *enmity* for your school?" she asked. "They do try so hard to teach you the foundational principles."

"They hate me there. I never learn anything. I don't want to go back."

Charlatan	(**shahr**-luh-tn) – N – a person who deceives by appearance
Imponderable	(im-**pon**-der-uh-buhl) – ADJ – not ponderable; cannot be determined
Junoesque	(**joo**-noh-esk) – ADJ – stately or regal (as a woman)
Enmity	(**en**-mi-tee) – N – a feeling of hostility

"It will be as you wish," Maleck's father said. "You've been expelled. It is a fitting punishment for the *foolhardy* stunt you played."

"I know. I'm sorry."

"Apologizing will not make the consequences go away," Azreel continued. "This will incur a punishment that you will not be able to mitigate with negotiations."

Maleck cringed. Here it came: the dire, awful, unthinkable punishment.

"We're going to *expatriate* you from the planet."

What? Maleck thought. *What does that even mean?*

Sensing her son's confusion, Beol interjected, "Military school—it's the only agreeable solution to your *knavish* behavior."

"I don't understand."

"The Earlmont Astrofleet Academy for Boys. It's on a ship orbiting the Trans System and is considered one of the finest institutions in all the Allied territories. It's perfect for you because there's no way to escape, except through the vacuum of space. Perhaps they can *inculcate* some behavioral norms into your stubborn head."

Although the idea of space travel had always intrigued Maleck, this journey did not seem like the adventure he'd always pictured. He was being sent to a prison ship to be locked away. This was going to be awful.

Foolhardy	(**fool**-hahr-dee) – ADJ – recklessly bold; foolishly rash
Expatriate	(eks-**pey**-tree-yet) – V – to banish (a person) from his country
Knavish	(**ney**-vish) – ADJ – untrustworthy; dishonest
Inculcate	(in-**kuhl**-keyt) – V – to implant by repeated statement; teach persistently

WORD REVIEW

Aplomb	Enmity	Inculcate
Belie	Expatriate	Interlope
Brazen	Foolhardy	Junoesque
Charlatan	Gamin	Knavish
Crony	Glacial	Notoriety
Defile	Iconoclast	Paean
Disaffect	Imponderable	Paragon

2

Maleck was already well-acquainted with the Earlmont Astrofleet Academy for Boys (EAAB), or at least had heard of its terrible *infamy*. Earlmont was used as a deterrent to keep children from doing bad things, not only by his parents. "I'll send you to Earlmont if you start behaving badly," had become a universal threat in households throughout the galaxy.

Therefore it's not surprising that a strong feeling of dread slowly started to *accrue* inside the soul of the punished youth as the space cruiser moved closer and closer to the enormous structure. Maleck watched through the window. Never had anything looked more like doom than the *austere* ship. The craft was black, almost invisible in the dark expanses of space. If it weren't for the small warning lights posted around its perimeter, it would appear like an unending shadow, permanently covering the bleakness.

His mother tried to *gild* the whole experience by telling him about the top-notch educational facilities, fully-equipped sports complex, and onboard art museum.

Infamy	(**in**-fuh-mee) – N – extremely bad reputation
Accrue	(uh-**kroo**) – V – to grow or add to in time
Austere	(aw-**steer**) – ADJ – severe in appearance; without ornament; serious
Gild	(gild) – V – to give a bright or pleasing aspect to something

Maleck was not to be fooled. Earlmont was not the type of institution one would brag about attending. This was a prison camp, no matter how you looked at it.

"One minute to dock," the driver said. "Brace yourself for landing."

At least his parents had the decency to hire a private taxi to escort him to his fate, rather than making him take the Earlmont passenger bus. Maleck would have hated making this journey in such close proximity to all the other knavish children. He enjoyed the opportunity to travel alone, and his parents gave him this consideration, although upon arrival he'd be forced to live in a shared community space.

The small space cruiser landed in the *gridiron* bay for small ships, basically a space parking lot. The driver opened the door for Maleck, and he exited. A Safety Officer waited for him.

"Maleck?" It was more of a command than a question.

"Yes. I am he."

The young Safety Officer nodded and pointed to Maleck's small bag.

"Are these your things?"

"Yes."

"You can't have them. I'll take them to the Locker until it's time for you to leave."

He yanked the bag from Maleck's person and started off. Maleck hesitated, and the young man immediately called over his shoulder.

"Follow me, or receive a *demerit*!"

Gridiron	(**grid**-ahy-ern) – N – any framework or network resembling a gridiron
Demerit	(dih-**mer**-it) – N – a mark of misconduct; fault

Maleck jumped to follow after him with *exigency*. This was his first day in an institution that could potentially house him for years. He wasn't going to mess this up. His plan was simple: forget all else, pay attention, obey commands, and get out early.

The Safety Officer was not much older than Maleck. He, too, looked to be a prisoner, but one who had found a way to rise above the ranks and receive extra privileges. He gave Maleck a tour as they walked.

"Over here is the recreation arena."

He pointed to a large, open arena filled with boys in uniforms competing in organized sports. Although fully indoors, it had the *façade* of being outside, with artificial sunlight, gentle breezes, and more. Maleck was impressed.

As they walked down the corridor, they were stopped by a *squadron* of marching boys. They walked in cadence, stepping together in perfect unison.

"Marching begins at 0500. Then there are drills throughout the day depending on your assignment."

As they waited, the youthful officer took the moment to give the new recruit a good once-over. He grimaced at Maleck with disappointment.

"You're kind of scrawny... Don't worry. After a few months here doing our daily strength exercises, you'll put on

---

Exigency	(**ek**-si-juhn-see) – N – urgency; situation needing prompt action
Façade	(fuh-**sahd**) – N – superficial appearance of something
Squadron	(**skwod**-ruhn) – N – persons grouped together for a similar purpose

some ***brawn***. Then you'll be decent enough. You're never fully a man until you can bench-press your own body weight."

The marching boys had passed, so the journey continued.

"Here are the dorms. It's two people to a room. Do you have your papers?"

Maleck handed over his assignment papers.

"Oh, 233B. That's funny."

"What?"

"You're with one strange cat... but you seem ***affable*** enough. Maybe you'll be the roommate that lasts."

The officer laughed at this remark, and began to open the door. Maleck didn't know if he should be excited or afraid to have a roommate of such infamy. No matter what, he knew he could handle it. He was never timid in new circumstances.

The door opened to reveal a small-framed boy sitting alone in the corner. His skin was pale, and his hair a stark white. In his hands he held a small blanket. The boy stroked the soft blue material lovingly.

"Your new roommate's here," the officer announced as he closed the door behind them.

The boy looked up to reveal a set of unmistakable eyes: one blue, the other green. A ***rarefied*** occurrence of traits that happens once in every million persons, Elihu—his new roommate—was completely unique. He continued to pet his blanket.

Brawn	(brawn) – N – muscular strength
Affable	(af-uh-buhl) – ADJ – friendly; easy to approach; pleasant
Rarefied	(rair-uh-fahyd) – ADJ – highly elevated; belonging to a select group

"Hello?" Maleck ventured. "I'm Maleck."

Elihu shook his head nervously, and backed away from his visitor.

"No. Me no like. Me want Mommy."

Maleck didn't know how to respond to his *atavistic* roommate who seemed to have reverted to a child-like state.

"Are you OK?"

Elihu motioned for him to come closer. As Maleck neared, Elihu threw off the blanket to reveal a small water gun. He squirted liquid into Maleck's face and began to laugh uproariously.

"Gotcha! You should have seen your face. You were so surprised!"

Having a naturally *gamesome* personality, Maleck joined in with the laughter. After all, as a practical joker himself, it would be hypocritical to hold such a prank against his roommate.

"You got me," Maleck said.

"I think the better description for such a great trick is that you got *bamboozled*," Elihu responded. "That's the official term, I think. Isn't it fun to say?"

"I like it."

"I'm Elihu, by the way. I live here."

"I live here now, too."

"Excellent. I think we'll be great friends."

Elihu put down his water-spouting contraption and jumped on the top bunk.

"This here's my bunk. You can have the bottom. Where are all your things?"

Atavistic	(at-uh-**vis**-tik) – ADJ – reverting to an earlier type; throwback
Gamesome	(**geym**-suhm) – ADJ – playful; frolicsome
Bamboozle	(bam-**boo**-zuhl) – V – to deceive; to perplex

"They took them," Maleck responded.

"Typical. They can be overly *autocratic* around here—just because they run the show. Don't worry. They'll give you some clothes and books before morning march."

Maleck looked around the small room, barely big enough for the two beds, a sink, a closet, and two desks. He thought it looked like a very clean prison cell, very manageable.

"Hey, have you ever heard of a Teleport?" Elihu asked.

"Only in fairy tales and conspiracy theories."

"They exist. I have one."

Not wanting to be a true *dupe*, Maleck didn't buy it. A huge fan of technology, he constantly read about the latest scientific innovations. The galaxy was light-years away from ever developing that sort of technology.

"Fool me twice, shame on me."

"It's the truth. I would never equivocate!"

"OK," Maleck responded. "Then show it to me."

"I can't. It's top secret. I can only use it by myself."

"Well, then I guess I just won't believe you."

Elihu smiled. He enjoyed the repartee with his new roommate. If this were an indication of things to come, the two of them were going to have a lot of fun. Elihu's *sanguine* expectations were matched by his incessant cheerfulness.

"I like you," Elihu declared gaily.

Suddenly they heard a loud buzz throughout the hallway and a *spate* of students filled the corridor. Hundreds of schoolboy feet shuffled beyond the door. Maleck looked to his roommate for clarity.

Autocratic	(aw-tuh-**krat**-ik) – ADJ – tyrannical; domineering
Dupe	(doop) – N – a person who is easily fooled
Sanguine	(**sang**-gwin) – ADJ – cheerful and confident; optimistic
Spate	(speyt) – N – a sudden outpouring

"It's dinnertime. Everybody needs to go to the mess hall."

"Shall we?"

"You go on ahead. I'll catch up... Go on!"

Although having no idea what to do or where to go, Maleck felt it *prudent* to be on his way. He would follow the other kids and learn by example. Surely they would all be going to the same mess hall. He'd figure it out.

Maleck exited his room and began following the boys in front of him. They traveled down one confusing corridor after the next until finally they reached a large open room full of tables and chairs.

Standing in the center of the room was Elihu, arms crossed and tapping his feet. He looked annoyed by Maleck's tardiness.

"What took you so long?" Elihu asked.

"How'd you get here so fast?"

"Teleport."

Not accepting this *spurious* account, Maleck responded, "Or you know a shortcut."

"Believe what you want, but I never wait in the *queue* for meals. I get here instantaneously. Now we have to wait in line because you took so long to get here. But I don't care because I'm your friend."

He motioned to a large line forming at the front of the mess hall. An army of boys were already waiting. Maleck and Elihu joined them. As they approached the line, they were immediately cut off by a tall Adonis-looking character

Prudent	(**prood**-nt) – ADJ – wise or judicious in practical affairs; careful in planning
Spurious	(**spyoor**-ee-uhs) – ADJ – not genuine or authentic; counterfeit
Queue	(kyoo) – N – a file for waiting in line; a braid of hair

named Xayx.

"Excuse me. We're in line," Maleck said.

"This spot belongs to a Bronze Medallion member," Xayx *swaggered* obnoxiously, "not losers."

Maleck began to fume, and Elihu couldn't help but begin to laugh.

"What's so funny?"

"Nothing… I can tell you're not the type of guy to let Xayx get away with acting like that."

"How is he in the Bronze Medallion? They're the most respected group of space explorers in the galaxy."

"His dad is a universe-renowned physicist, who took Xayx on an exploratory expedition that made huge scientific discoveries. The whole crew received the honor… Xayx included. He's here because they're grooming him to be the next Ambassador."

"I'm sure an obnoxious guy like Xayx in politics will help create a *utopian* universe," Maleck said sarcastically. "That's all we need is more people like him messing things up!"

"Hey, aren't your parents in government?" Elihu questioned Maleck.

"How do you know that?"

"I work in the administrative office. I do research on every recruit."

"That doesn't seem legal," Maleck responded, unnerved.

"It's not. I know a guy who's an exceptional computer hacker. Nobody finds out."

Swagger	(**swag**-er) – V – to walk or strut; to boast noisily
Utopian	(yoo-**toh**-pee-uhn) – ADJ – resembling utopia; involving idealized perfection

"OK... Well, it's true. My parents hold *sinecure* offices in Acritas; they barely do anything but tell people what to do."

Elihu began to laugh out loud.

"What's so funny?" responded Maleck.

"You still don't believe me about the Teleport, huh?"

"No way."

"I need you to watch me."

Elihu smiled at Maleck, and headed off toward the other end of the mess hall. Maleck watched as his new friend exited the room and walked out of sight. Then he felt a tap on his shoulder. Maleck turned to find Elihu standing right behind him.

"Hello," Elihu boasted.

Stunned, Maleck stood there with his mouth agape. There's no way he could have *prognosticated* that unlikely result.

"How did you... That's impossible!"

"Now, watch this!"

Elihu turned around and ducked under a nearby table. Almost instantly, there was another tap on Maleck's shoulder. He looked back amazed to find Elihu once again standing near him.

"It's me again," Elihu stated *nonchalantly*, as if appearing and disappearing at whim were no big deal.

"But the laws of physics... and... there's no way that...

Sinecure	(**sahy**-ni-kyoor) – N – an office or position requiring little or no work
Prognosticate	(prog-**nos**-ti-keyt) – V – to predict; to prophesy
Nonchalant	(non-shuh-**lahnt**) – ADJ – coolly unconcerned or indifferent; casual

I can't believe…" Maleck was incapable of being *articulate* after witnessing such a marvel.

"It's OK, buddy," Elihu interjected. "I'm sure this must be hard for you."

"HOW DID YOU DO IT?" Maleck demanded.

Elihu signaled for Maleck to quiet and move in close. He spoke in a hushed voice.

"Not right now. This place is too *populous*; we need to be somewhere private. We can talk about it in the room tonight. But for now, let's keep it quiet."

"Wait, didn't anybody else see this?"

Elihu laughed in response. "These people are dumb as bricks! They don't like to think about things they don't understand. Even if they saw me use the Teleport, they wouldn't believe it… Quiet, OK?"

Maleck nodded obediently. This was the greatest discovery of his life. When he got his food, he could barely eat. He just sat and wondered about the Teleport. *How big was it? Who made it? How did Elihu get it?* The questions were overwhelming. He couldn't believe how it didn't even seem like a big deal to Elihu. Maleck watched him laugh and joke and eat, and nothing seemed to faze him.

Later that night, Maleck was forced to wait outside the room as Elihu got everything ready to showcase. Never had he felt more impatient in his life. He would be one of the first in the universe to see such a *prodigious* device, and more impressive, if everything went according to plan, use it!

Articulate	(ahr-**tik**-yuh-lit) – ADJ – uttered clearly; having clarity and effectiveness
Populous	(**pop**-yuh-luhs) – ADJ – crowded; full of residents
Prodigious	(pruh-**dij**-uhs) – ADJ – extraordinary in size; wonderful or marvelous

Finally Elihu opened the door, and Maleck leaped inside. He walked around the room expectantly looking for the Teleport. Seeing nothing out of place or new, he paused.

"Where is it?"

Elihu backed against the closet and held fast the doorknob.

"It's in here."

"Come on already," Maleck demanded *petulantly*. "Let me see."

"OK, but promise to control yourself."

"I will."

Hesitantly, Elihu opened the closet door as slowly as he could. Standing in the closet was another Elihu, or at least a boy who looked exactly like Elihu.

"Surprise! I'm the Teleport," the new boy ventured.

"I don't mean to be mendacious," Elihu added, "but it's just so much fun to play these tricks!"

So many emotions swirled around in Maleck's brain that he didn't know what to think. Anger, confusion, disappointment, excitement—they were all such good choices to express at this moment. He landed on anger, and thus the *altercation* began.

"What's the big idea?!? Do you think this is funny? I don't. Very stupid. I ought to punch you both!"

"Don't be so *querulous* and whiny," Elihu demanded. "It's not a big deal. You're just a little gullible."

"Gullible? How I was supposed to know you two are… what? Identical twins or clones or something?"

Petulant	(**pech**-uh-luhnt) – ADJ – showing impatient irritation
Altercation	(awl-ter-**key**-shuhn) – N – a heated or angry dispute
Querulous	(**kwer**-uh-luhs) – ADJ – full of complaints

"Twins," replied the other brother with total *equanimity*, for the argument had not roused him at all. "I'm Darden."

"We're not actually identical though," Elihu added. "Our eyes are different."

Upon further examination of the brothers, Maleck could see that although they both had one green eye and one blue eye, they had them in reverse order.

"Oh, yeah, of course. How silly of me," Maleck stated. "How could I fall for such a silly trick?"

"Don't worry—not even our parents can tell us apart sometimes," Elihu replied.

"Our mom has a *mnemonic* device to help her remember. Maybe it'll help you. 'Left eye blue is Elihu.' Then of course the other twin is Darden... that's me."

"I'm the smart one," Elihu added.

"I'm the dumb one," Darden continued.

"I don't care!" Maleck *chided* them, still fuming mad. "You shouldn't do that to people! Is this some kind of secret, or is this just a joke you played on me?"

"Everybody knows about us," Darden explained. "We were just fooling you. I live on a different floor. We use the air ducts to go back and forth."

"You seemed like such a good sport!" Elihu said trying to *inveigle* his roommate into calming down. "You are intelligent, with a great sense of humor, and you've got great taste in literature and art..."

"How do you know that?"

Equanimity	(ek-wuh-**nim**-i-tee) – N – calmness; equilibrium
Mnemonic	(ni-**mon**-ik) – ADJ – assisting memory; pertaining to mnemonics or memory
Chide	(chahyd) – V – to express disapproval; to nag
Inveigle	(in-**vey**-guhl) – V – to ensnare by flattery

"We do our research," Darden added. "I'm the expert hacker who got your files, but hacking is the only thing I'm good at."

"The truth is…," Elihu stammered, "we really want to be your friends, and we would like to offer this prank as our formal application to hang out with you."

Although Maleck normally wasn't susceptible to flattery, and although he could see right through Elihu's scheme to gloss over the prank, Maleck decided to succumb to their offer of friendship. Truth be told, he had been looking for friends like Elihu and Darden all his life— pranksters with a disregard for proper procedure. Now that they had found each other, there was no telling what sort of shenanigans they could drum up. Let the mischief begin!

WORD REVIEW

Accrue	Exigency	Prudent
Affable	Façade	Querulous
Altercation	Gamesome	Queue
Articulate	Gild	Rarefied
Atavistic	Gridiron	Sanguine
Austere	Infamy	Sinecure
Autocratic	Inveigle	Spate
Bamboozle	Mnemonic	Spurious
Brawn	Nonchalant	Squadron
Chide	Petulant	Swagger
Demerit	Populous	Utopian
Dupe	Prodigious	
Equanimity	Prognosticate	

3

A t 0500, the entire student body of Earlmont would *amass* in the sports complex and stand in formation. Although he had only been there a few weeks, Maleck had already developed a distaste for waking up early. This routine would be his fate until the end of his sentence at the military academy. At least today was Friday, and that meant all the students could dress casually. Not wearing a uniform was Maleck's only consolation for being awake.

On large screens across the domed facility, the Drill Sergeant blasted out orders for the morning. His *stentorian* voice bellowed through the ranks of boys, causing shivers down the spines of the weak. Maleck was not afraid. In fact, his mind was very far away from marching orders this morning. His attention was focused on Xayx only a few rows in front of him.

Maleck loathed Xayx. The guy was a *surly* bully to everyone, especially the smaller and younger boys. He spit gum on the floor, tripped people walking down the halls, and one time even poured iced milk down Elihu's back.

Amass	(uh-**mas**) – V – to collect; to come together
Stentorian	(sten-**tawr**-ee-uhn) – ADJ – very loud or powerful in sound
Surly	(**sur**-lee) – ADJ – churlishly rude; unfriendly or hostile

Maleck had had enough of this *blowhard*, and today he was going to do something.

He watched as Xayx chatted with his friends, ignoring the strict silence policy during morning practice. Maleck was annoyed. He tried to shush them.

"Hey! Quiet down."

Xayx responded with a look of condescension.

"I can't hear!" Maleck continued.

Laughter was the only response Xayx could muster.

"What was that, new kid?" Xayx *chortled* with a sneering grin. "Why don't you go back to your room and cry about it?"

This response angered Maleck even more. Fortunately for him, the plan to teach the bullying churl a lesson was already in progress. The twins, Elihu and Darden, were at this moment deeply *embroiled* in creating the best payback in the history of the school.

Both twins were exempt from marching orders. Their parents were quite *impecunious*, so they didn't have the money to pay the large tuition cost of Earlmont. Therefore both boys had to work in the school facilities department during non-school hours. This afforded them many advantages in gaining access to areas otherwise forbidden to students.

Their days were very routine. Each of them made the same rounds every day, taking the same pathways, and passing each other in exactly one spot. On this morning,

Blowhard	(**bloh**-hahrd) – N – a boastful and talkative person
Chortle	(**chawr**-tl) – V – to chuckle gleefully
Embroil	(em-**broil**) – V – to throw into confusion; to bring discord
Impecunious	(im-pi-**kyoo**-nee-uhs) – ADJ – having little or no money; poor

they dressed exactly the same because their confused identity was essential to the success of their plan.

As Elihu left the headmaster's office he met Darden in the corridor. Normally the two boys shared a wave at this juncture, but today Elihu handed a small package to Darden, who was on his way to the institution control room. Nobody noticed the hand-off.

Darden opened the package and unwrapped a key. He placed the key in his jumpsuit pocket and continued walking. Every room in the facilities department was access-restricted by time of day, and only Darden had access to the control room in the morning. When he reached the control room, he placed his hand on a scanner to gain entrance. Although none of the staff could tell the difference between the twins, the computer always knew.

Inside was another small office for the headmaster. It also served as a broadcast booth for all of his school-wide announcements. This door was not restricted by handprint, merely a simple lock. Darden was not allowed in this room, but his brother Elihu could enter on special occasions, serving as the headmaster's liaison. Darden placed the key in the door, and as he was about to enter, a guard appeared.

"Hey, what are you doing?"

Darden immediately assumed the *guise* of his twin brother.

"I'm Elihu Fencaster. I work for the headmaster."

The guard began looking through his roster of authorized personnel. He found Elihu's picture, and compared it to Darden. Fortunately the guard was too

---

Guise   (gahyz) – N – general external appearance; assumed appearance

imperceptive to notice any difference between the two brothers, so he allowed him to pass.

"OK. You're clear."

Darden entered the room, and immediately began hacking into the broadcast computer. He uploaded a file and set a timer delay for broadcast. The new video would *interpolate* the regular announcements by adding a new segment of the daily updates. If this prank worked, he'd be breaking every *ordinance* established by the school authorities, but he didn't care. It would be well worth it.

When finished, he exited the computer and tried to erase all proof of his presence in the room.

* * *

It was lunchtime, and Maleck intentionally sat by himself in the mess hall. This would be a moment to remember, and he wanted to savor it alone.

In the center of the room, he watched Xayx sitting in a *grandiose* pose at the table, barking orders at his minions. He looked like a king lording over his tiny *fiefdom*. It didn't take long for the tyrant to notice Maleck's stares. In a huff, he marched over to his table.

"What do you want, *new kid?*" he demanded.

"Nothing. Just observing the wildlife."

Imperceptive	(im-per-**sep**-tiv) – ADJ – lacking perception
Interpolate	(in-**tur**-puh-leyt) – V – to introduce between two things
Ordinance	(**awr**-dn-uhns) – N – a command; a public regulation
Grandiose	(**gran**-dee-ohs) – ADJ – affectedly important; pompous
Fiefdom	(**feef**-duhm) – N – domain of a feudal lord

"Listen here, you don't have the *mettle* to mess with me."

"Are you calling me a coward?" Maleck retorted.

"I'm saying you're chicken. That's why you sit here alone, watching... too afraid to face me like a man."

Maleck stood, ready to take on the challenge.

"Here I am. If you want to fight, let's go."

Xayx approached, fist raised. He knew instinctively that he'd really enjoy beating Maleck into the ground. As he neared, the screens in the mess hall suddenly went live. Everyone looked up. Video footage began to play of Xayx in his dorm room, holding a stuffed zebra and petting it lovingly.

"I wub you, wittle zebwah... I wub you," he said in babytalk.

Xayx shook his head violently, "NO! How did they get this? Turn it off! Turn it off!"

Immediately, laughter *pervaded* at every table of the mess hall. Maleck smiled, as Xayx became flustered, looking around the room frantically.

"Stop it! It's not funny!"

Then the video skipped, and transitioned to a video of Maleck and the twins planning the prank. When Darden was uploading, he had accidentally included footage from his personal video diary. It was undeniable proof that Maleck was involved in the prank; there would be no way for him to *disclaim* his involvement. He was in big trouble. Xayx turned to Maleck with a sinister grin. Maleck's skin turned *sallow*, and he felt like he was going to vomit.

Maleck stood up, and sped with urgency away

Mettle	(**met**-l) – N – courage and fortitude; temperament
Pervade	(per-**veyd**) – V – to spread throughout all parts
Disclaim	(dis-**kleym**) – V – to disown connection with; to deny
Sallow	(**sal**-oh) – ADJ – of a sickly or yellowish color

from Xayx. As fast as he could, he crossed the hallways and ran toward his bedroom. It was the rendezvous point for the three pranksters after the event occurred. Hopefully, the twins would already be there waiting for him.

Xayx stayed close on his heels. In fact, as Maleck turned the corner, Xayx was able to grab his shirt. Maleck pulled with all his might and managed to break free, all the while ripping his sleeve.

As he continued running, Maleck managed to knock a trashcan on the ground, spilling garbage on the floor. This gave him enough time to make it to his room and lock the door behind him. The sound of Xayx banging on the door came almost immediately.

"I'm going to kill you! Just wait till I get in there!" Fortunately for Maleck, the twins were already waiting for him inside.

"What do we do now? What's the plan?" Maleck asked hurriedly.

"I don't know," Darden responded. "Getting found out was not part of the plan."

"Well our involvement in this is *manifest*, not only to Xayx, but also to the school staff," Elihu said, "which means we could get into some serious trouble. Maybe even detention for years. They'll make an example of us!"

"What do we do?" Maleck queried.

"There's only one way out of this *predicament*... escape!" Elihu said. "There's an air duct under the bed. Darden and I use it all the time to get into each other's

| *Manifest* | (**man**-uh-fest) – ADJ – obvious; apparent |
| *Predicament* | (pri-**dik**-uh-muhnt) – N – an unpleasantly difficult situation |

rooms. Let's go to Darden's room!"

"But then what?"

Loud feet came rushing to the door outside. The Safety Officer's voice bellowed down the hallway.

"Open up, right this instant! They are on their way with the keys, so it'll be better for you to do this willingly."

Elihu opened the vent and motioned for Darden to enter.

"What we'll do when we get there is **appurtenant** to the more important issue of escaping this room right now."

Maleck nodded in agreement and jumped into the air duct. His hands pounded on the cold metal as he crawled behind Darden. Elihu followed them and replaced the vent cover from the inside. Ting...Ting...Ting... the sound of crawling echoed through the passageway. There would be no surprise as to where or how they had escaped. Anyone with ears could follow them to Darden's room.

When they finally arrived, Maleck was more than nervous. What a horrendous **calamity**! Now they would get in trouble for two things: their prank and trying to escape. *How stupid! You can't escape a space ship!*

"Now what are we supposed to do? They'll come here looking for us next."

"I don't know," replied Darden.

Elihu took a moment to cogitate. He squeezed his face together and almost turned red. Then, all of a sudden his eyes lit up.

"I got it!"

"What?"

Appurtenance	(uh-**pur**-tn-uhns) – N – something subordinate to a more important thing
Calamity	(kuh-**lam**-i-tee) – N – a great misfortune; affliction

"Darden, the evac pods are down the hall, right?"

"Yeah!"

"Let's escape there!"

"No way!" Maleck *balked*. "I'm not leaving this ship to get spit out in the middle of space."

"That's not what I meant," Elihu demanded. " They have windows so we can observe the guards. We can hide in there, at least until the heat dies down."

"Then what?"

"I don't know, but we can figure it out from there. Are you coming or not?"

"OK," Maleck replied *dyspeptically*, "I guess it can't get any worse."

Elihu placed his hand over his mouth and motioned for the others to be still. He placed his ear against the door, and then quietly opened it. The hallway was empty of guards, so Elihu went out. Carefully, Darden and Maleck followed. The boys ventured to the chamber of evac pods. Then all of a sudden, the alarm began to sound and the emergency lights started to flash.

"Attention all staff! Be on the lookout for Maleck Vise Plutean, Elihu…"

"Quick!" Elihu commanded. "Get in!"

He pressed a large red button on the launch pad and the door opened to the closest pod. The boys quickly jumped in. Almost immediately guards were running about the hallway *en masse*. Maleck watched as the group of guards scattered about and searched the rooms in the confusion caused by the loud alarm, lights, and shouting.

Balk	(bawk) – V – to stop and refuse to proceed
Dyspeptic	(dis-**pep**-tik) – ADJ – gloomy or pessimistic; pertaining to dyspepsia
En Masse	(en **mas**) – N – all together; as a group

The evac pod, in contrast, was completely soundproof, a *cloister* of peace from the confusion.

Thinking about how much trouble they were in, Maleck gave his friends a look of disappointment. He attempted a half-hearted smile.

"Well, at least we have a few moments to ourselves," he said. "I think what's most important is that when they find us, we stick together and maintain *solidarity*. If we all tell them the same story, nobody will get singled out. I think everybody will get a lesser punishment."

"I don't want to get into trouble at all," Darden said.

"You know," Elihu pointed to the launch box, "this can get us away from the ship... No, that's stupid. We'd be lost in space... but maybe lost in space is better than being in trouble for the rest of our lives... but we could die in space..."

"Enough," Maleck commanded, annoyed by Elihu's silly, *capricious* thoughts. "We're not going anywhere. We'll eventually just have to give ourselves up."

"Yeah, you're right," Elihu said as he pressed the launch button to *instigate* takeoff. The pod made a quick jerk and threw the boys onto the floor. The launchpad began to circle and then finally ejected the pod from the Earlmont ship. After a loud buzzing sound they began to float free in outer space.

"What did you do?!?"

"The only thing I could do. I saved us."

Cloister	(**kloi**-ster) – N – a quiet, secluded place, esp. for religious purposes
Solidarity	(sol-i-**dar**-i-tee) – N – community of purpose; having unity
Capricious	(kuh -**pree**-shuhs) – ADJ – indicative of whim; erratic
Instigate	(**in**-sti-geyt) – V – to urge or provoke

"We're going to be killed!"

"Look!" Darden interrupted. Out the window was a red planet that seemed to be inching its way closer and closer. "We're falling toward that planet!"

"See, we're in that planet's orbit," Elihu began his pretentious *bombast*. "That was my plan all along. Escape to that planet."

"That's not true at all," Maleck *dissented*. "How do we even know that it's suitable for human life or that it's even more than gaseous matter?"

"Don't worry, my dear Maleck," he countered. "We're in the Revandry System. Almost 80 percent of the planets are suitable for human life."

"So then there's only a 20 percent chance that we'll die just by landing on this planet."

"Exactly."

Maleck could not believe Elihu's *myopia* in embarking on such an adventure without thinking about possible problems. Landing on this planet could be extremely dangerous, and the gravity of the situation was lost on him.

As the pod moved nearer and nearer to the planet's atmosphere, Maleck began to brace himself. Red lights flashed like fire along the pod windows, and the whole vehicle began to shake. He closed his eyes tightly and clenched his teeth. If they were going to crash, he didn't want to watch... And that was the last thing he could remember.

Bombast	(**bom**-bast) – N – pompous speech; pretentious words
Dissent	(dih-**sent**) – V – to disagree; to differ in opinion
Myopia	(mahy-**oh**-pee-uh) – N – lack of foresight; narrow-mindedness

WORD REVIEW

Amass	Dyspeptic	Mettle
Appurtenance	Embroil	Myopia
Balk	En Masse	Ordinance
Blowhard	Fiefdom	Pervade
Bombast	Grandiose	Predicament
Calamity	Guise	Sallow
Capricious	Impecunious	Solidarity
Chortle	Imperceptive	Stentorian
Cloister	Instigate	Surly
Disclaim	Interpolate	
Dissent	Manifest	

4

Maleck woke up, surrounded by the ***dross*** of their wrecked space vehicle. Surprised to even be alive, he slowly managed to raise himself up. There was a crick in his neck from sleeping in a weird position or falling hard... he wasn't quite sure what had happened.

Shiny metallic fragments of the evac pod littered the crash site. One large piece trapped Maleck's leg. He gently picked the ***ferrous*** spaceship debris off his limb and threw it to the side. With both hands, he inspected the leg for injuries—totally fine. Other than feeling a small bit of neck pain, Maleck was relatively unharmed.

Where in the universe are we?

For the first time Maleck took the opportunity to observe his surroundings. The land was bare. Dark red soil covered the plain with no signs of vegetation. They had crashed into a valley. High rocky mountains encircled them with ***precipitous*** cliffs, ominous and probably impossible to climb over.

Maleck felt a pang of dejection. *Why had he listened to the twins? Why did he get into the evac pod? Would they ever find a way out of here?*

Dross	(dros) – N – waste matter; refuse
Ferrous	(**fer**-uhs) – ADJ – containing iron
Precipitous	(pri-**sip**-i-tuhs) – ADJ – extremely steep; characterized by precipices

This was not a planned excursion in the slightest. They didn't have food. They didn't have water. They didn't even have a map! Nor did any of them have a clue where they were at that moment. His thoughts turned to Elihu and Darden. Anger against their reckless *temerity* began to rise up inside him. This whole thing was very stupid. In frustration, Maleck looked out toward the landscape.

What are we supposed to do now?

Maleck watched as *eddies* of wind blew dust in the air like small tornados. He thought it was a prophetic sign of their impending doom.

"Morning, chap!" a voice came from behind.

Maleck's two comrades appeared, awake, chipper, and loudly *garrulous*.

"We've been exploring! It's so cool here!"

"There are quite a number of interesting mineral formations and some unusual stone structures. The whole expedition has been quite enjoyable," Elihu continued.

"I wish I would have brought my camera. It's like every place is a great photo op!"

Finally, they realized that Maleck still remained lying on the ground. He, unlike them, was not overwhelmed by the excitement of their new adventure.

"You're on the ground... are you hurt?" Darden queried.

"No," Maleck replied. "I'm just a little shaken up."

"Then get up, lazy bones! We've got so much to do."

"We need to make a plan," Maleck declared. "There are so many things that we need to take care of."

Temerity	(tuh-**mer**-i-tee) – N – reckless boldness; rashness
Eddy	(**ed**-ee) – N – a small whirlpool; a trend counter to the main current
Garrulous	(**gar**-uh-luhs) – ADJ – excessively talkative; wordy

"We can worry about that later," Darden replied. "Do you realize the epic game of Akseg we can play here? There's so much empty space!"

"Stop goofing off!" Maleck demanded. "This is serious!"

"What made you so *peckish*?" Elihu questioned with a disappointed frown. "Everything will be taken care of. We've already made a plan, and the plan allows for playtime."

"When did this happen?"

"We held a *plebiscite* to determine what we should do. We voted and determined that finding a source of food and water although important, could wait until later. You were there... don't you remember?"

"I was unconscious!" Maleck retorted. "You can't say I voted if I wasn't awake—my personal *suffrage* has been violated!"

"Don't worry. The plan to move forward passed by a wide majority. Your vote wouldn't have mattered any way."

"That's not fair. You two are twins! You have the same brain."

"No," Darden interjected. "I'm a lot dumber."

"Whatever! I had no choice in the matter."

"OK," Elihu conceded. "You're right. Why don't you offer a suggestion and we can vote on its merits."

"Good!"

Maleck finally got to his feet. He brushed off his clothes assertively and looked around. Their evac pod had

---

Peckish	(**pek**-ish) – ADJ – rather irritable; somewhat hungry
Plebiscite	(**pleb**-uh-sahyt) – N – a vote to decide an important decision
Suffrage	(**suhf**-rij) – N – the right to vote; a vote given

landed on a central *promontory*, high above the rest of the valley. This gave the boys an unencumbered view of their location. There was nothing in the near distance that could help them sustain life. They would have to venture into the unknown. Perhaps they could find civilization of some sort, or if nothing else, water.

Maleck *abhorred* the idea of leaving the crash site, where almost certainly a rescue team would be sent after them, but the best plan would be to go searching for essentials.

"It seems prudent to seek out supplies immediately." Maleck decided.

Elihu shook his head in thoughtful agreement.

"Well, then. I guess it's settled." Elihu declared. "We shall go in search of life-sustaining necessities right away."

"We should lead," Darden added, "because we've already been exploring."

"Go ahead."

The boys set off on their journey, following in a straight line. The terrain was orange and rocky. Rocks seemed to jut up out of nowhere and fill the landscape. This forced them to take a rather *circuitous* path around the stark cliffs and crags scattered throughout.

As much as Maleck disliked being shipwrecked on an unknown planet, he began to realize the *aesthetic* appeal of the interesting place they had discovered. Two suns appeared in the sky, or maybe two moons—he couldn't

Promontory	(**prom**-uhn-tawr-ee) – N – a bluff or plateau; a high point of land in the sea
Abhor	(ab-**hawr**) – V – to regard with extreme disgust; detest
Circuitous	(ser-**kyoo**-i-tuhs) – ADJ – roundabout; not direct
Aesthetic	(es-**thet**-ik) – ADJ – pertaining to a sense of beauty

tell the difference—which bathed the planet in a beautiful auburn glow. The rock formations, although difficult to walk around, gave the land a unique beauty. It was as if the minerals themselves had a personality and couldn't be confined to the ground; they had to jump into the air to be seen by the lost hikers.

It wasn't long, however, before Maleck began to suffer from the *privation* of food and water. The last time he had eaten was in the mess hall when Xayx chased him out. His plate was left half-full, and Maleck was accustomed to eating two or three servings per meal. All three boys were naturally *hale*, but a lack of food and water would eventually turn them weak and sickly.

After traversing most of the valley, it was pretty clear that no food or water would be found unless they ventured beyond the mountains. Then Maleck noticed a passageway in the heights. Out of the large barrier of rock surrounding the valley, one mountain dipped low in front of them. Perhaps salvation could be found on the other side?

"Guys, we should try for the pass in the mountains. It may take us somewhere promising." Maleck offered.

"You're right," Elihu responded. "Rescue ships from Earlmont won't make it here for hours, maybe even days. Planets in this district are known for crazy, carnivorous animal life. We need to find shelter. Remaining *static* in this valley would surely mean an untimely death. Let's head there immediately."

Privation	(prahy-**vey**-shuhn) – N – lack of the usual comforts; act of depriving
Hale	(heyl) – ADJ – free from disease; vigorous
Static	(**stat**-ik) – ADJ – fixed in a stationary condition; showing little or no change

That's when Maleck realized this was Elihu's plan all along, which immediately irritated him. Why didn't he just say that they were leaving the valley in the first place? Did he think Maleck would be unduly obstinate?

"Why not tell me we were headed this way in the first place?" Maleck retorted.

"I only dissembled the plan because we couldn't afford to have you disagree. I figured it would be much better if you came up with the idea yourself."

"Am I that contrary? I deserve more credit."

"Our chances of survival in this desolate valley are *infinitesimal*; we couldn't afford for you to disagree."

"I knew this was the plan all along," Darden added, "because I agree with everything."

Maleck sighed. Arguing would only prove to be *futile*; there was no point. They all knew their only option would be to try to make it out of the valley.

The pathway began to incline as they got closer to the pass. The steeper it got, the more Maleck began to feel the lack of food. He wasn't weak necessarily, just feeling the need to eat.

The three boys stopped when they finally reached the *genesis* of the pass, unsure about entering the narrow corridor. Sharp rocks protruded from both sides of the opening. It looked dangerous and uninviting. To make matters worse, the mountains rose so high above it that there was no sunlight on the pathway. It was dark and covered in shadows. As they looked deep inside it, they could tell it would only get

Infinitesimal	(in-fin-i-**tes**-uh-muhl) – ADJ – infinitely small; minute
Futile	(**fyoot**-ul) – ADJ – frivolous; ineffective
Genesis	(**jen**-uh-sis) - N - an origin or beginning

darker the farther they went.

"I don't like this," Maleck concluded. "This seems wrong."

"Yeah," said Darden. "I'm scared."

"Look, we have two options," Elihu declared. "Either we die of starvation or try to conquer the scary passageway."

"Maybe we should wait until we're sure there's nothing for us here. Besides, I bet the people at Earlmont are looking for us. If they're going to find us, we should stay by the evac pod. "

"It's in our best interest to make this journey while we still have some strength," Elihu countered. "And Earlmont will never find us. It's not like we're lost in a park or something. We crash-landed on a planet! It could take them years to locate us."

"You're right," Darden said, always Elihu's loyal *adherent*. "We should move forward."

The boys began to move. Elihu entered first. Being the *de facto* leader meant he had to face the dangers head on. Not that there was a formal vote or anything; he just assumed the role. Maleck had no way of opposing this hierarchy due to Darden's full-hearted support of everything his brother did.

Elihu got a sudden chill as he entered the pass. Having no direct sunlight caused the temperature to drop significantly. Darden and Maleck followed close behind. They watched as their breath turned white in the cold. Maleck touched the freezing wall and discovered *hoarfrost*

Adherent	(ad-**heer**-uhnt) – N – a person who supports a cause; a follower	
De Facto	(dee **fak**-toh) – N – in fact; in reality	
Hoarfrost	(**hawr**-frawst) –N – frost; a covering of minute ice needles	

on his fingertips.

As they continued down the passage, a strong gust of wind *blustered* through the passageway, causing the boys to shiver. The howling noise was eerie. It sounded angry and ominous, as if the passageway itself was commanding the boys to turn around.

Darden stopped suddenly, frozen in fear.

"Wait!" he called out. "Do you hear that?"

The other boys stopped as well. They listened to the wind. In the distance behind them they could hear a strange panting noise, like a creature huffing and puffing in motion. But it wasn't coming from inside the cavern, it was originating from the way they came. Something was headed their way, and whatever it was, it was about to trap them.

"Move! Move! Move!" Elihu screamed, and the three boys took off, pushing themselves farther and farther forward.

As they ran, the sound of footsteps pounded behind them like horse hooves in a race. Maleck couldn't resist looking over his shoulder. That's when he saw the *hirsute* monster chasing them. It was twice the size of any horse he'd ever seen, with long shaggy hair that covered its eyes. Its face was wide with ominous sharp teeth and green slobber dripping down from its mouth. The creature looked hungry, and Maleck had no intention of becoming lunch.

The animal moved swiftly with *insuperable* speed. No matter how fast the boys ran, it would soon overtake them. They needed a plan, or at least a way out. That's

Bluster	(**bluhs**-ter) – V – to be loud, noisy; to roar, as wind
Hirsute	(hur-**soot**) – ADJ – hairy; shaggy
Insuperable	(in-**soo**-per-uh-buhl) – ADJ – incapable of being beaten

when Maleck spotted an opening in the rocks ahead. It was a small crevice, barely large enough for a human. If it led to a cave or at least a hole big enough to fit three, it could potentially be their salvation.

"Look!" Maleck exclaimed. "There's an opening. Try to get in it!"

Elihu darted for it as quickly as he could. The space was barely large enough for his body, but he was able to wriggle his way inside. Maleck and Darden followed with the creature dangerously close behind.

The sounds of its breathing grew louder and louder. Darden entered first, then Maleck, but Maleck was a little bigger. He struggled to fit through the crack. Just as the monster reached his legs, he pushed through, barely avoiding his *nemesis*. The teeth of the creature bit and chomped at the opening, attempting to break through the hole, but to no use. The three boys were safe.

Maleck paused with a sigh of relief, but immediately noticed a small flicker of light. They landed in a cave, which already had occupants. As he moved toward it, it became clear that a small fire flashed and danced down the passageway. This was more than a cave. It was a *silo* of some sort, created for storage. Silently the three boys pushed forward until they spotted a shadow approaching them. It was disproportionately large and threatening. They were not alone.

Nemesis	(**nem**-uh-sis) – N – something that cannot be conquered; a rival
Silo	(**sahy**-loh) – N – a structure that stores food or missiles

WORD REVIEW

Abhor	Futile	Peckish
Adherent	Garrulous	Plebiscite
Aesthetic	Genesis	Precipitous
Bluster	Hale	Privation
Circuitous	Hirsute	Promontory
De Facto	Hoarfrost	Silo
Dross	Infinitesimal	Static
Eddy	Insuperable	Suffrage
Ferrous	Nemesis	Temerity

5

As the shadow approached them the three boys *mustered* together in preparation for another battle. After all, they had just survived the attack of a huge, hairy monster. They knew if they stuck together they could take on any challenge.

The shadow came closer and closer, and in so doing became smaller and smaller. It definitely had the shape of a person. When the being finally turned the corner, the shadow was no bigger than Maleck or the other boys.

The apparition was nothing more than a young girl. She was beautiful by all common standards—slender, pale, and with dark eyes that seemed to pierce directly to the heart.

"It's just a girl!" Darden sighed. "We were afraid for nothing."

Elihu was not so easily relieved. "Who are you?" he questioned.

"My name's Alystra," the girl said as she stroked her flowing black hair. "Who are you?"

"I'm Elihu. This here's Maleck and my brother Darden. We're lost."

"Are you hungry?" she questioned. "I'm cooking food right now."

Muster   (**muhs**-ter) – V – to gather together; to assemble for battle

"Boy howdy!" Darden exclaimed.

Alystra returned to the fire and the boys followed her. They entered a large chamber that had been set up for living. There was bedding and some chairs, rudimentary but livable. Beside the fire was a *larder* of food. This girl had enough stocked up to last for months.

"It is very *munificent* of you to share with us," Elihu commented suspiciously.

"It's no bother. I have plenty for myself, and I shouldn't be here long enough to finish all of it."

"Where are you going?" Maleck asked. "Or better yet, where are we?"

"We're in a cave," she said sarcastically. "You boys look like foreigners. This is the planet Silva."

"You mean Planet Exile?" Elihu questioned.

"Some people call it that. Nobody who lives here would. We're a very *libertarian* society; we have few laws, and almost no policy or standards on immigration. We get the name 'Exile' because we welcome individuals who have a hard time going anywhere else."

"You mean like outlaws and riffraff," Elihu concluded.

"In a way, yes. That's kind of how my troubles started," she began to *chronicle* her background. "My father is the Administrator of Silva."

"You mean like the president?" Maleck asked.

"Yes, kind of like the president in terms of function, but he's not elected by the people in a democratic way. In

Larder	(**lahr**-der) – N – pantry or supply of food
Munificent	(myoo-**nif**-uh-suhnt) – ADJ – very generous
Libertarian	(lib-er-**tair**-ee-uhn) – ADJ – advocating liberty or free will
Chronicle	(**kron**-i-kuhl) – V – to record as in a chronicle

fact, voting on Silva is quite impossible. There are so many different beliefs and opinions that consensus can never be reached. Every attempt has had political leaders *gerrymandering* districts and so much corruption that we just stopped the process all together. It's much better for us to have one ruler, who just makes all the decisions, as long as that person is noble and honest. The Administrator of Silva is more like a king in that his title and power are *bequeathed* to him."

Darden's eyes began to twinkle. "You're like a princess!"

"No, I wouldn't go that far," she responded. "I'm not next in line or anything. Power is passed down to the most worthy person, regardless of family connections. I'm just a normal girl."

Darden, ignoring her denial of royalty, exclaimed, "Wow, a *bona fide* princess!"

"So if you're a princess," Elihu questioned incredulously, "then why are you hiding in a cave?"

"My father was *deposed*, and now they're trying to kill me."

"Who would want to kill you?" asked Maleck.

"His successor, Roman Belaynee."

"Who's that?"

"A criminal. Belaynee thinks that somehow I can start a revolution, but I'm just a kid. He's one of the many ne'er-do-wells who come to our peaceful planet and try to

Gerrymander	(**jer**-i-man-der) – N – dividing voting districts to favor a certain party
Bequeath	(bih-**kweeth**) – V – to hand down; pass on
Bona Fide	(**boh**-nuh fahyd) – ADJ – made in good faith; authentic
Depose	(dih-**pohz**) – V – to remove from office; to affirm under oath

cause problems. It's no wonder why they are not welcome in other societies. All they do is cause problems."

"How did he take control?"

"Belaynee possesses a lot of *charisma* and can get people to follow him" she said. "He has this natural way of attracting people. After only a few months, he was able to muster up a significant number of followers."

"But what does that matter?" Elihu asked "You just said that your planet doesn't vote."

"When Belaynee found that out, he was outraged. He gathered his followers and they marched all the way to the Administration Courts. They demanded that my father *abdicate* his position of power. When he refused to swear *allegiance* to Belaynee's group, they locked him up in prison."

"So, you ran away."

"I was sent away, actually. My father knew something was going to happen when the rabble approached the courts. Our housekeeper packed a vehicle full of living materials, and then swept me off to the middle of nowhere... which is where we are now."

"How long have you been here?"

"It's hard to say. Not too long, I don't think. I've completely lost track of time. I've had absolutely no contact with the outside world since that *demagogue* took over and started stirring up the people. He's a tyrant. Anybody who opposes him gets imprisoned or worse... and all the criminals go free! It's terrible. He's the leader

---

Charisma	(kuh-**riz**-muh) – N – special ability of leadership or popularity
Abdicate	(**ab**-di-keyt) – V – to renounce or relinquish the right
Allegiance	(uh-**lee**-juhns) – N – loyalty to a person or group
Demagogue	(**dem**-uh-gog) – N – a person who gains power by arousing emotions

only because he knows how to appeal to the desires and opinions of murderous–"

Alystra stopped herself, realizing that she had begun to get heated. As a proper lady, she always tried to maintain a gentle spirit. She apologized since she couldn't believe how her emotions had become so ***effusive***.

"I'm sorry. I let myself get a little carried away. Come. You boys must be starving. Let's eat."

The girl moved effortlessly to the fire where several pots and pans had been set up on a grate. The living quarters were fully equipped with everything Alystra would need for a several-month stay, but her father had failed to plan an ***egress*** for his daughter. It seemed almost like a fairy story of old—a princess locked away in a cave, waiting for somebody to save her. But who would be her Prince Charming? If Darden had his way, it would be him for sure. He knew he could beat the other boys in a race to her heart, if either gave him a challenge. But first things first—they must eat.

Inside the big pot was a sweet-smelling stew, unlike anything the boys had smelled before. The young girl served them each a bowl, her soft hands gracefully pouring the soup. Although unaccustomed to manual labor, Alystra was still able to maintain a state of extreme elegance and poise in everything she did.

The boys ate and ate and ate. After they finished the stew, she served bread with dipping sauce, followed by a purple pasta dish. Although unappealing in appearance,

Effusive	(ih-**fyoo**-siv) – ADJ – unduly demonstrative; lacking reserve
Egress	(**ee**-gres) – N – exit; the right to go out

it was undeniably delicious. The food *cloyed* the boys to the point of exhaustion. Maleck ate so much that he felt like his stomach would explode.

"So, Princess…" Maleck said. "I have a question. How do you go to pooper in this cave?"

Alystra responded with a shocked face, a little perturbed by the *crass* way in which Maleck spoke. She didn't like slang very much.

"We have a fully functioning waste disposal unit," she responded. "But I'm not going to ever use it again. I'm planning to escape. A supply ship comes every six months or so and heads directly to the Peacekeeping Commission. My plan is to sneak onto it."

Maleck gave one quick look at Alystra, and knew her plan was doomed to failure without the intervention of his band of brothers. There would be no way for her to "sneak" onto anything. Even without her silky white gown trimmed by fine *ermine*, her very demeanor would give away her upper-class upbringing.

"Good thing we're here," Maleck stated. "Otherwise you never would have made it."

"What a horrible, execrable thing to say!" she contended. "I'm just as capable as any boy!"

"I'm sure you are… and I'm sure they're looking for you. Do you think they would let any girl of your age walk around without getting challenged? If anyone's on the lookout, the moment you set foot in public, you're caught."

Cloy	(kloi) – V – to weary by an excess of food or pleasure; to satiate
Crass	(kras) – ADJ – without refinement; gross
Ermine	(**ur**-min) – N – white fur, esp. to identify royalty or high rank

"I know. You're right," she relented. "That's exactly why I haven't gone out yet. It's too hard to do alone."

"Listen... Alystra, right?" Maleck queried. She nodded in affirmation.

"You have a *patrician* air about you—your aristocratic clothes, the polite way you speak, the cleanness of your skin. If you're going to sneak onto some space ship, we've got to change everything about you. Now, when you said sneak onto a ship, did you mean like get on it anonymously or fly without paying?"

"Oh, heavens! I would definitely pay! I have plenty of money."

"Perfect. It's much easier to disguise you than it would be to get a free ride on a space ship... although it can be done," Maleck laughed.

"That sounds wonderful, but unusually generous. You'll be risking your lives. Are you hoping to gain *lucre?* Because I do have money..."

"You're too pretty to pay us," Darden said.

"We would love to help you for free, if it helps us get to safety as well. Elihu, help this woman look more like a man!"

"A man! No one said anything about dressing like a man! That's a horrid *abomination!* My father would never approve."

"Your father would rather you be alive in disguise than dead... Besides they'll be looking for a girl, not a boy," Maleck responded.

Patrician	(puh-**trish**-uhn) – ADJ – aristocratic; like a person of high rank
Lucre	(**loo**-ker) – N – monetary reward or gain
Abomination	(uh-bom-uh-**ney**-shuhn) – N – a vile, shameful action or condition

"The first thing we need to do is change your clothes. You need something *careworn* and dirty… something like…" Elihu spotted an old blanket on the couch, "Like that!"

Elihu walked over to it and shook it in the air. It was covered in cave dust. The fabric was blue and thick like a nice pair of work pants. He rubbed it into the dirt a bit for good measure.

"Darden," Elihu commanded. "Find something to cut with… We're going to make this fine maiden a pair of trousers."

As Darden rapidly pieced the pant legs together, Alystra directed Elihu to her clothing trunks. He rustled through her belongings until discovering a thick winter coat. It had a very masculine design, almost military in nature. He also found a winter scarf. When the work trousers were finished, Elihu was certain all the items together would create a pretty convincing disguise. When Alystra put them all on, she actually appeared to be a sloppy and *slovenly* 12-year-old boy.

Elihu shook his head disapprovingly. "There's a problem—a big one."

"What?" Alystra questioned.

"You're too clean. One look at your face or your hands…"

Elihu grabbed her hands and turned the palms upward. Soft and white, they would immediately give away her cover. They weren't *calloused* or toughened at all. Scornfully, Elihu dropped her hands and pointed her to the ground.

Careworn	(**kair**-wohrn) – ADJ – showing signs of care or worry
Slovenly	(**sluhv**-uhn-lee) – ADJ – untidy or unclean in appearance; slipshod
Calloused	(**kal**-uhs) – ADJ – hardened; insensitive

"I need you to rub your hands in the dirt."

Reluctantly, Alystra did as she was instructed. Her face grimaced as she touched the dirt-covered floor.

"Now get it in your fingernails. That's the telltale sign of authenticity... if it's in the fingernails."

Alystra obliged.

"Now rub dirt on your face."

She began to panic. This unexpected command was more than a little *disconcerting* to her. Alystra took such care to keep her face clean. The very idea of placing dirt on her face was appalling. Elihu attempted to comfort her.

"Don't worry. It'll wash off. Everything will be OK."

Slowly, but surely, Alystra lifted a dirty finger to her spotless cheek. She dabbed a spot of brown. She did this again, and again, until finally she was brave enough to cover her whole face in soil. After a moment of accepting her fate, she began to calm down.

"You look great!" Elihu commented. "Perfect, even. I would never recognize you. There's just one last thing to do."

"What?" she asked timidly.

"Your voice. It's too delicate and proper. Everything you say is so *eloquent*, like a refined queen. I need you to sound like a stupid, gruff boy."

"I've already gone this far. What must I do?"

"Speak in short sentences, with one or two words... Try 'Hey, you!'"

"Hey, you," she responded timidly.

"No, no. That's too light. People will see right

| *Disconcert* | (dis-kuhn-**surt**) – V – to perturb; to disarrange |
| *Eloquent* | (**el**-uh-kwuhnt) – ADJ – having or exercising the power of fluent, forceful, and appropriate speech |

through it. I need you to say it with conviction. Loud enough that the *stalactites* hanging in the back of the cave can hear you. Try again."

"Hey, you!" she shouted.

Elihu smiled. His creation was complete. No one would recognize this poor work-hand boarding a ship to the Peacekeeping Commission.

"I think you're ready."

Stalactite   (stuh-**lak**-tahyt) – N – a deposit hanging from the roof of a cave

WORD REVIEW

Abdicate	Cloy	Gerrymander
Abomination	Crass	Larder
Allegiance	Demagogue	Libertarian
Bequeath	Depose	Lucre
Bona Fide	Disconcert	Munificent
Calloused	Effusive	Muster
Careworn	Egress	Patrician
Charisma	Eloquent	Slovenly
Chronicle	Ermine	Stalactite

6

Prairieton, Silva. This small town was once the *phoenix* of morality and order of the entire planet. That was, until Roman Belaynee took over. Chosen as the home base for his political operations, within a matter of weeks this former symbol of decency had become a *decadent* playground for the wayward kind, hosting all manner of activity from gambling to fighting to smoking and chewing.

Although it may have seemed a little foolhardy for the kids to venture into enemy headquarters, the supply ship for the Peacekeeping Commission made only one stop on Silva, so Prairieton was their only shot of escape. Known for having diplomatic relations with even the most unfriendly territories, the Peacekeeping Commission was famous for its ability to grant safe passage to all types of refugees. In the most extreme cases, it even provided military support in violent situations.

To any onlooker, the three boys and one girl appeared to be four boys. Alystra was instructed to keep quiet and speak only when absolutely necessary. This was a command she had no problem obeying, for she became increasingly more frightened as they neared the small

---

Phoenix   (**fee**-niks) – N – a person or thing of beauty; paragon
Decadent   (**dek**-uh-duhnt) – ADJ – characterized by cultural or moral depravity

town. The loud sounds of laughter and frivolity blustered toward them as they approached.

By the time they reached the city, it was midday, and people were running wild. From afar, they could see the main street crowded with rabble-rousers. A big group of men fought in the street, almost aimlessly hitting each other and the people around them. It was *anarchy* with nobody taking charge, nobody telling anyone to stop. Passersby paid no mind to the commotion, as if it were an everyday affair.

As the group approached Prairieton, they were struck by a fetid odor. Alystra couldn't help but cover her delicate nose.

"Yuck!" Darden exclaimed. "It stinks here."

A mountain of trash was piled outside the front of the town. Since the start of the demagogic *regime* of Roman Belaynee, no one had cared to take out the garbage. In fact, there were a lot of everyday necessities that had been ignored by their new leader. It seemed as if the new governing philosophy of the region had become "all play and no work," and it was evident by the horrible smell.

Besides being *delinquent* with the trash, the new government had overlooked a few other important factors... mainly laws. A society based on complete freedom in a location occupied mainly by a criminal population was a dangerous combination. For Maleck, the situation was eye-opening. All his life, he had detested

---

Anarchy	(**an**-er-kee) – N – a society without government or law
Regime	(ruh-**zheem**) – N – system of government; government in power
Delinquent	(dih-**ling**-kwuhnt) – ADJ – neglectful of a duty; overdue

the rules and ordinances forced upon him by society as a whole. "Don't fight... Don't spit... Don't throw your trash on the ground..." It all seemed like such hogwash—old people just trying to confine him. But here and now, he started to see the picture a little more clearly. If everyone threw their trash on the ground, you would end up with a stinking pile of garbage unpleasant for everybody—citizens and visitors alike.

As the four travelers entered the main road, the place appeared even more chaotic. Prairieton was made up of one main *esplanade* going through the center of the town. Old-time storefronts made of wood and gray shingles lined the street. It was the Wild West, or at least an incarnation so closely resembling the outlaw frontier that it could have been a time warp.

The pathway was narrow, which made the expanse of people seem even crazier. As the kids walked through the mess, they were barely able to avoid the activity swooning about them. At first, Maleck almost walked into the play of a dice game. A group of men were throwing dice, and one die flew out of their circle onto the pathway where Maleck was about to walk. Fortunately, Maleck saw the misplaced die and avoided stepping on it. An angry-looking man walked up to Maleck and picked up the gambling piece.

"Two. The die rolled two." He stared Maleck straight in the face. "Good thing you didn't step on it, boy, or I would have punched your lights out."

He shook his fist in Maleck's face and walked away. Maleck swallowed hard and realized that a world full of

---

Esplanade   (**es**-pluh-nahd) – N – any open, level space, especially for a public walk or drive

anomie was a chaotic world he didn't want. People here had no morals or any qualms about doing whatever they wanted, no matter who got hurt in the process.

Suddenly, a loud siren sounded from the center of town. It was announcing the presence of Roman Belaynee. The townspeople immediately moved toward a large stage set up with streamers and speakers, showing their *fanaticism* with shouts and applause. They seemed to worship their newfound leader for providing them with the society of pure selfishness.

People began to fill the streets in even greater numbers. Maleck, Elihu, Darden, and Alystra crowded together. They wouldn't let this onslaught of people separate them. In the process, they were forced to get closer and closer to the stage. Three police vehicles flew into the town square and parked in the dirt. (Although reminiscent of olden-days, Silva only had vehicles that flew or hovered.) Then he appeared, the man of the hour. Roman Belaynee had a hard, weathered face. He wore a mustache and black cowboy hat. His clothes were worn, but elegant. He looked almost like an ancient army general or president.

"Ladies and gentleman," he started. "Thank you for joining me on such an *august* and magnificent day as today. Why is today so special, you ask? This marks the one month anniversary of our revolution!"

The crowd began to clamor with excitement. Alystra rolled her eyes at his pomposity, "Such a *braggart.*"

Anomie	(**an**-uh-mee) – N – the breakdown of social norms and values
Fanaticism	(fuh-**nat**-uh-sahyz-uhm) – N – fanatical character and spirit
August	(aw-**guhst**) – ADJ – venerable; eminent
Braggart	(**brag**-ert) – N – a person who brags a lot

"Shhh!" Elihu warned. "Be careful." Alystra nodded her head apologetically.

"The complete *dissolution* and abandonment of all laws works! We have a properly functioning society, and it's all thanks to you—the people! In honor of this important occasion, we've bought out the entire Blue House Saloon. Spend the day in celebration; drinks are on me!"

The crowd exclaimed joyfully. Belaynee exited the podium, and he started to lead the crowd toward the drinking establishment. En masse, the people began walking behind him. Love him or hate him, Belaynee had a magnificent way of leading people. They seemed to *obsequiously* follow his every word.

The four adventurers stayed put, allowing the crowd of people to wash over them and move forward. Soon the area was quite empty. They had a moment to themselves for the first time since entering Prairieton.

"He was cool," Darden said.

"That's all they need, more reasons to be indolent. These people are already as lazy as can be, and this just encourages their *inert* nature. All they do is goof off!" Alystra remarked.

"Whoa!" Elihu added. "We need to be careful of bitter and *censorious* remarks! We have no idea who could be listening. You don't have to like what's going on, but

Dissolution	(dis-uh-**loo**-shuhn) – N – the undoing or breaking into parts
Obsequious	(uhb-**see**-kwee-uhs) – ADJ – showing servile deference; obedient
Inert	(in-**urt**) – ADJ – inactive or sluggish
Censorious	(sen-**sohr**-ee-uhs) – ADJ – severely critical; fault-finding

save your negative comments until we're safely aboard the ship to the Peacekeeping Commission."

Alystra nodded apologetically. Elihu was right. Strange eyes and ears were all over the place. They couldn't risk letting the wrong person overhear them. Maybe it was already too late. At the corner of one of the buildings, a woman was beckoning them.

"Kids! You kids! Come over here!" She said.

"What do we do? Run?" Elihu questioned.

"I think we should go to her," responded Darden. "She looks nice."

"We could always outrun her if she's up to no good. Let's go, but Alystra, stay in the back."

The group timidly moved closer to the woman. They had no idea what they should expect. Friend or foe, this woman could be a great ally or great enemy. She waved her arms urgently, trying to get the children to move with more haste.

"Hurry! Hurry now!" she said. "Come inside here, now!"

The woman ushered them into the side door of a large old-fashioned hotel. They entered a small living quarters, as an offshoot of the main building. It was quaint, with a kitchen, table, and single bed.

"Now, you children shouldn't be playing outside in Prairieton!" she *exhorted* sternly. "It's not safe around here. Come, let Auntie Matilda help you."

Matilda was a kind-looking woman, beautiful, with a *corpulent* figure and matching round face. Her chubbiness only added to her friendly demeanor. If the

---

Exhort	(ig-**zawrt**) – V – to urge; advise; caution
Corpulent	(**kawr**-pyuh-luhnt) – ADJ – fat; portly

group had any fear, it almost instantly melted away the moment she began talking.

"I've lived here close to my whole life, and never have I seen it like this!" she continued. "People acting so crazy. The streets are dangerous. There's fighting here, and debauchery over there. It's no place for children. We need to get you out of here as quickly as we can!"

"Well, we're actually trying to get out." Maleck said. "That's our plan, anyway, to fly out of here."

"I knew it!" she exclaimed. "I had a feeling this morning, a *premonition* that I'd be meeting you. I knew there'd be some kids in trouble, and my gut just told me to go outside and look for you. And there you were!"

"We need to get to the shipyards. There's a flight going out to the Peacekeeping Commission that we need to make."

"Oh, I see. That's a little farther south from here. The road there is very dangerous. I would never walk there if I were you. A bunch of robbers and thieves lie in wait for any victim who comes their way. They'll get you children for sure."

"What do we do?" Darden asked.

"Let's see here… Every day I got to make my rounds of deliveries for the hotel. I don't normally go down that way, but I could pretend to have something that needs to go down there. You kids can hide in the back of my cruiser… See, I used to be a space captain myself, in the Royal Army. I was a religious officer. I have a few connections down there still."

"That's rather a meritorious favor to make for some strangers," Elihu mentioned suspiciously. "Most people don't do such nice things without having an ulterior motive."

Premonition   (pree-muh-**nish**-uhn) – N – a forewarning; antici-
                    pating a future event

"Well, I guess I just have the natural *inclination* for helping people. It's not that much trouble and I like to do it… so I guess my motivation would be the fact that I will enjoy it."

"Then we appreciate the offer," Darden concluded.

The four kids looked at each other, leery. It seemed like the best thing for them to do would be to trust Matilda to take them to the shipyards, but it could also be some sort of a trap. Either way… they didn't have a choice.

"Besides," Matilda added. "I hate to think of you children wandering around in such a vile, *reprobate* place as this. Who knows what could happen to you? There are people who would stop at nothing to get what they want. They don't care how young you are."

Matilda instructed the group to wait until she was able to get her deliveries ready, and then they would head off to the shipyards.

After Matilda left them alone, the kids *loitered* around the apartment for what seemed like hours. It was hard not to think that she wasn't coming back, or maybe the whole thing was a trap. But as the sun began to set, sure enough, Matilda came back and hustled them all into her cruiser.

The vehicle was small, but it had several storage compartments in the back. Each adventurer received his own private compartment to hide in until they reached their destination. They were instructed not to speak or make any noise during the journey, and they were all obliged to obey.

Inclination	(in-kluh-**ney**-shuhn) – N – a preference; state of being inclined
Reprobate	(**rep**-ruh-beyt) – ADJ – morally depraved; unprincipled
Loiter	(**loi**-ter) – V – to linger aimlessly; to move in a slow manner

The portly woman drove under the cover of night. The dark road adequately hid the vehicle from prying eyes. At night the population in Prairieton was found exclusively in saloons or casinos. This was the best time to travel. There was nobody in sight. It seemed as if this plan would work flawlessly, until Matilda spotted a blockade of flashing lights in front of her. Although Belaynee's administration was known for inefficiency and the inability to get things done, they still were able to manage an *impromptu* road inspection every now and then. Sometimes in the middle of the night, they would decide to show up and stop vehicles. They just wanted an excuse to harass people.

"Where are you going?" an officer demanded of Matilda.

"The shipyards. I'm making a delivery."

"What are you delivering?"

Matilda reached into a bag next to her and *adduced* a small package, labeled to a company in the shipyards, for she had anticipated the possibility of such a stop and was ready for it.

The officer walked around the cruiser suspiciously. He began to bang on the compartments with his stick. He stood above Alystra's storage unit and tried to open it, but it was locked.

"Can you open this compartment for me?"

This question sent a fit of fearful *ague* surging down the young girl's spine.

Impromptu	(im-**promp**-too) – ADJ – made without previous preparation; improvised
Adduce	(uh-**doos**) – V – to bring forward in argument or as evidence
Ague	(**ey**-gyoo) – N – a fit of fever, shivering, or shaking chills

"Oh, you know what?" the woman said. "I lost the key to that a few months ago. It's somewhere in my apartment, I know it. I just don't have any clue what I did with it. I get so confused some times. Honestly, I don't even remember what's in there. I think maybe blankets or animal feed? I don't much remember."

"Never mind," the officer said, and casually left the compartment alone. "I guess that'll be all."

"Thank you, sir, for keeping us all safe," Matilda exclaimed as she drove past the barricade. Escaping their trip's *encumbrance*, she let out a sigh of relief.

"We're all clear, kids," she cried out to the back.

The space cruiser finally arrived at the Prairieton Shipyard, which half-resembled a space-age bus station. Matilda went to the storage compartments and released the *itinerant* children at their final stop on their journey across the planet Silva.

They were universally filled with *jubilation* at having arrived safely. Alystra was ecstatic. She could go to the Peacekeeping Commission and have someone come back to save her father! Darden was the only person not overjoyed by their arrival. Elihu, having a *congenital* ability to sense when his brother was distressed, looked to him, concerned. Twins often have such telepathic connections.

"What's wrong, Darden?" he asked.

"I have to go the bathroom!"

Encumbrance	(en-**kuhm**-bruhns) – N – something burdensome; hindrance
Itinerant	(ahy-**tin**-er-uhnt) – ADJ – traveling from place to place
Jubilation	(joo-buh-**ley**-shuhn) – N – a feeling of festive celebration
Congenital	(kuh n-**jen**-i-tl) – ADJ – existing from birth; inherent

This exclamation made everyone laugh.

"It's over around back," Matilda instructed. "They don't do nothing fancy here. You gotta walk out to the pot... Now kids, just go on inside and buy your tickets. I'm afraid I'm going to have to leave you here. This trip is going to make my deliveries go late. I can't afford to be any later. I would stay with you all night if I could."

Maleck stretched out his hand to shake Matilda's hand. "Thank you for all your help. We appreciate it."

The woman shooed away his hand and grabbed him for a hug. She hugged all three of the kids—only three for Darden had immediately rushed to the toilet after finding out where it was. With a sweet smile, she returned to her vehicle and drove away.

Together, Maleck, Elihu, and Alystra entered the shipyard's main building. It was filled with rows and rows of benches occupied by bored and *listless* citizens waiting for their flights. They all appeared so tired and spiritless.

At the front was a counter with two lines, one for passengers and one for *mercantile* customers, for the shipyards often shipped both people and goods. The travelers got into the passenger line.

"I'm so excited," Alystra exclaimed. "We're almost there!"

"But we're not there yet," Elihu warned.

When they reached the front of the line, Maleck took control.

"We need four tickets for the ship bound for the Peacekeeping Commission."

Listless	(**list**-lis) – ADJ – having little interest; spiritless
Mercantile	(**mur**-kuhn-teel) – ADJ – of or pertaining to merchants; engaged in trade

"OK." The customer service representative looked through his log and got out four tickets.

"That'll be 586 gram-units."

Alystra offered the money willingly, and the man exchanged the tickets.

"All right. Come back on Saturday."

"What?" Alystra cried out.

"The ship doesn't arrive here for another three days. Didn't you check the schedule?"

"There must be something you can do!" Alystra exclaimed in her full female intonations. "You have no idea who my father is!"

Suddenly, a voice came booming from behind them.

"Princess Alystra, we've been looking for you."

The foreboding sound of the voice caused the small girl to *cower* in fear. Slowly the three kids turned around to find an imposing-looking officer standing over them.

"You're under arrest."

Cower (**kou**-er) – V – to crouch, as in fear

WORD REVIEW

Adduce	Decadent	Itinerant
Ague	Delinquent	Jubilation
Anarchy	Dissolution	Listless
Anomie	Encumbrance	Loiter
August	Esplanade	Mercantile
Braggart	Exhort	Obsequious
Censorious	Fanaticism	Phoenix
Congenital	Impromptu	Premonition
Corpulent	Inclination	Regime
Cower	Inert	Reprobate

7

A portly man in full cowboy attire sat at the gate of the jail cell. The prison was an old building made of sullied wood *dappled* with holes. It seemed like it was originally built for temporary use, but had for years been used extensively. The morning after the children's arrest, the building was busy with activity. Soldiers rustled about the surroundings putting on boots and preparing their weapons. For some reason, it seemed as if the whole platoon was being deployed.

The three children sat alone in a cell designed for 30. They were completely surrounded by steel bars, close enough together that nobody could fit though. Maleck knew this because Alystra had already tried, and even her slender frame was too thick.

"All right, Gene," a soldier said to the prison guard. "You make sure those kids don't get away."

"Yes, sir," he responded gaily. Gene took a moment to look at his three captives and smiled. In his right hand he *burnished* a shiny, silver-barrelled laser gun, polishing it with a cloth in a manner that implied a readiness to shoot anybody who attempted escape.

Dapple   (**dap**-uhl) – N – a spot or mottled marking
Burnish   (**bur**-nish) – V – to polish; make smooth

The children watched as the man stood and paced back and forth from the posterior to the *anterior* part of the room, trying to intimidate them. As the other men filed out of the building, Gene seemed to gain more confidence in his steps. By the time everyone else had gone, he had perched along the wall, and just stood there, watching them, completely happy to have free reign to do whatever he pleased with his prisoners.

The way in which Gene maliciously watched them *begot* in Alystra an overwhelming sense of fear. It wasn't just that she was the only girl of the group and smaller than the boys; as the Administrator's daughter, she was also a political figure representing her father's regime. From history, she had learned that the princes and princesses were always the victims of slaughter after any sort of power change. Since the people of Silva often saw her like royalty, she could foresee a future including the chopping block!

"We've got to get out of here," she whispered to Elihu as she watched the guard.

"Why?" he responded *complacently* with a shrug. "This isn't so bad. They give us great food." Elihu had a steel plate full of country fixings like mashed potatoes and fried okra, which he chomped on voraciously. She moved to Maleck, who was fortunately endowed with the same sense of fear.

"Maleck! What are we going to do?"

"I don't know." Maleck thought for a moment,

Anterior	(an-**teer**-ee-er) – ADJ – placed in the front; coming before
Beget	(bih-**get**) – V – to cause; produce as an effect
Complacent	(kuhm-**pley**-suhnt) – ADJ – pleased and unaware of danger

and then made an ***impetuous*** jump. "I'm going to talk to him."

"Hey!" he called out. "What's going on here? Where'd everybody go? Why are you all by yourself?"

Gene took a good, long look at Maleck and rolled his eyes. Maleck's multiple questions served to harry the man into a response. With every step, he chewed Yilisin, a purple grass native to Prairieton. He shot a wad of spit on the floor and approached the boy ominously.

"Although it ain't none of your business," the man started, "they're taking care of the Administrator."

"What do you mean?"

"Going to get everybody together at noon, and drop the fella into the Cherkle Den. Belaynee's taking the warship out there."

"What?!?" Alystra exclaimed from the other side of the room. She rushed over to him and began to plead through the bars. "You can't do that! You can't! That's insane! It's not fair! Please stop it!" The girl almost immediately broke into hysterical tears.

"If you think cryin's gonna make me go easy on you, you're wrong." Gene was one of the strictest guards of all the prison keepers; ***laxity*** was an appalling idea to him.

Maleck, confused, looked to Elihu. "Cherkle?"

"That monster that chased us into the cave... that's a cherkle. They like eating people. I learned about them in my planetary biology class. So I ***construe*** that a cherkle den is a cave full of cherkles."

Impetuous	(im-**pech**-oo-uhs) – ADJ – moving with great force; a sudden, rash action
Laxity	(**lak**-si-tee) – N – state of being loose or lenient
Construe	(kuhn-**stroo**) – V – analyze and explain a phrase, especially in connection with translating

"You're a genius," Maleck responded, unimpressed by Elihu's obvious logic. "What are we going to do about it?"

Elihu waved his hand in the air like a regal magistrate and walked over to the prison guard, who had returned to his post of polishing his weapon and watching the kids.

"Excuse me!" he said. "I would like a word with you."

The man didn't move.

"You're not the *gregarious* type I see, but I, on the other hand, like to talk. I can be twice as gregarious for the both of us!"

Nothing happened again. Elihu was going to need something more exciting and interesting to break through Gene's silent *carapace*. Then the idea hit him. Why didn't he think of it before?

"Have you ever heard of a Teleport?"

Gene looked up, interested but suspicious.

"Because I got one," Elihu continued. "It's real and it works."

"What're ya talkin' about, boy?"

"I can jump from one spot to the next, almost magically. I can teleport pretty much anything in the world!"

This was enough to make Gene walk over to the boy. "I've heard the stories," he responded. "But I haven't seen anything with my own eyes. It's my personal *credo* to wait to see something before I'll believe it."

"Well, you'd better get ready to believe, because I have a good mind to use it to get out of this jail cell."

Gregarious	(gri-**gair**-ee-uhs) – ADJ – fond of others; sociable
Carapace	(**kar**-uh-peys) – N – a bony shell; shield
Credo	(**kree**-doh) – N – any creed or formula of belief

* * *

Darden felt an overwhelming sense of relief in the lavatory room outside of the shipyards. He had been waiting, waiting, and waiting. He had first felt the urge to go before Matilda picked them up, long before, but he didn't want to miss the ride, so he kept it to himself and held it until they arrived. He could hold it no longer and finally discovered the long-awaited relief.

Darden knew something was wrong almost immediately when he approached the main building of shipyards. This feeling was **accentuated** by the rapid onset of flashing lights and military vehicles. He watched as his brother, Maleck, and Alystra were boarded into a van and locked inside.

He had no idea what to do, but at the same time knew exactly what needed to be done. Although this incongruity might seem like an **oxymoron**, for Darden, it was how he was designed. Being the dumb side of a two-headed coin, he was used to living by his feelings. It's how the twins worked together. Darden would have the feeling to do something, and Elihu would figure out how to make it work. At this moment, Darden knew he had to rescue his friends. He just didn't know how.

As the van carrying the prisoners drove away, Darden simply and easily grabbed onto the side and hitched a ride. This was a very common practice in Silva because there were so few vehicles driving around. Most drivers paid little attention to their attached riders, and Darden was not alone

---

Accentuate	(ak-**sen**-choo-yet) – V – to make more noticable; to emphasize	
Oxymoron	(ok-si-**mawr**-on) – N – a figure of speech that seems self-contradictory	

in hanging on the side. There were also several city **marshals**, helping escort the vehicle back to the jail.

Darden was nervous the whole ride. Surely somebody would notice that their hitchhiker resembled one of their prisoners identically. For that reason, Darden huddled himself into his jacket and refused to make eye contact. Fortunately for him, Silva was playing Reductor in the Tournament Bowl that night, and every officer was tuned into the game and tuned out of their environment. A few other stragglers hung on the vehicle as well, so Darden didn't stand out in any way.

The prison was located all the way back in the center of Prairieton, where the four kids had started their journey. As they neared the building, Darden quickly jumped off before they made a complete stop. He took the opportunity to run as far away into the distance as possible, while still being able to maintain a clear view of the fate of his friends. He watched as all three were led into the jailhouse, and presumably locked up.

What was he to do now? It was time for him to think for himself for once. Across the street was a saloon called Crazy Pete's, one of the many that littered the streets of the small town. The exterior had a mural of a corpulent man with crazy eyes drinking kegs of moonshine. This seemed like the perfect place for some quiet thinking.

The place was alive when Darden entered. People crowded around the main stage as a group of lady singers performed amateurish versions of old classics. Darden headed straight to occupy the one lonely spot at the bar.

Marshal   (**mahr**-shuhl) – N – military officer; sheriff

Pete, the eponymous bartender, didn't seem crazy at all. He had an *avuncular* demeanor, like a favorite uncle. He smiled at Darden as he walked up. He didn't often see youngsters in his establishment, but Darden's presence didn't surprise him. Everything had been crazy since the rise of Belaynee. A kid in the bar was just another way in which the town was falling apart.

"What can I get for you?" he said with a smile.

"Pop! No, water. No, whiskey. No! Water." Finally, Darden had decided; he was not used to being so *fickle*, but he also wasn't used to thinking. It was much harder than it appeared.

The bartender came back with his drink, and set it down politely.

"There'll be no *corkage* fee on that; water's free."

Darden began to sip his water pensively. Pete, noticing the rabble occupying the bar, gave the wayward boy a compassionate look.

"I've got some advice for you, kid," he said.

Looking for anything to help him, Darden focused intently and listened with *sedulous* ears. Maybe this random bartender could solve all his problems.

"A boy your age shouldn't be in a place like this. Look around. See all these folk in here. You don't want to be like them, *indigent* and jobless. You don't want to end up broke and drunk all your life, son."

Avuncular	(uh-**vuhng**-kyuh-ler) – ADJ – characteristic of an uncle
Fickle	(**fik**-uhl) – ADJ – likely to change, esp. due to caprice
Corkage	(**kawr**-kij) – N – a fee charged for serving wine in a restaurant
Sedulous	(**sej**-uh-luhs) – ADJ – diligent in attention; assiduous
Indigent	(**in**-di-juhnt) – ADJ – poor; impoverished

"You're right," he responded. "That's good advice, but not really what I'm looking for."

"What's going on? Tell Uncle Pete."

"My brother's in trouble. He's been caught up by bad people. I want to help him, but I don't know how."

"Ah," Pete responded. "Problems of the *fraternal* kind—let me tell you that brothers can be hard at times, but they're worth the hassle. Maybe you guys have a mutual friend who could talk to him. Set him straight a little bit."

Darden thought a little and then remembered Matilda. Maybe she could help him.

"I do know somebody," Darden confessed, "but how do I know if I can trust her?"

"Son, people will tell you a lot of things, and most of that stuff ain't worth its salt. They say they're your friend or your buddy, but it don't mean nothin'. When somebody shows you who they are by their actions, that's what you should believe."

Fraternal   (fruh-**tur**-nl) – ADJ – brotherly; befitting brothers

WORD REVIEW

Accentuate	Construe	Impetuous
Anterior	Corkage	Indigent
Avuncular	Credo	Laxity
Beget	Dapple	Marshal
Burnish	Fickle	Oxymoron
Carapace	Fraternal	Sedulous
Complacent	Gregarious	

8

B *ereft* of any other options, Darden stood outside the hotel where Matilda worked considering his only apparent choice. It had been only a few hours since his friends had been captured, but it seemed like an eternity from when Matilda had dropped them off. He did not want to put the fate of himself or his brother in the hands of a complete stranger—for all he knew, Matilda could have tipped off the authorities about their arrival to the shipyards. But there were no other options.

With hesitation, he approached the side door. By this time it was late at night. She was probably fast asleep, if she even lived in the little room in the first place. Darden had no idea. In fact, at no time specifically did Matilda mention that the hotel quarters were her place of residence. Some big scary criminal could answer the door—but he knocked nonetheless.

Thump... Thump... Thump...

All his fears were **abrogated** by Matilda's familiar appearance at the door. Half-slumbering, she wore a nightgown with her hair in a bun. A look of deep concern crossed her face as soon as she recognized the small boy at her doorstep.

"Come in, child," she said, hushed. "Hurry."

Bereft   (bih-**reft**) – ADJ – deprived
Abrogate   (**ab**-ruh-geyt) – V – to abolish; to put an end to

Her genuine look of surprise and overall friendliness allowed Darden to trust that Matilda had been *forthright* from the beginning. He even felt a tad guilty for doubting her.

The *incandescent* light of a small ionic crystal lantern gave the room a soft, silvery glow. It was warm like the home of a grandmother. She motioned for Darden to take a seat, as she shook her head in amazement.

"What happened, son? What's going on? Oh dear!"

"I had nowhere else to go..."

"You're lucky I even opened the door—you know, I'm not *predisposed* to answering it in the middle of the night. Who knows who could be knocking? All types of vagrants come around these parts."

Matilda had multiple *strictures* for the citizens who occupied Prairieton that loitered about during the wee hours of the night, but she decided to hold her tongue in front of Darden. Her utmost goal was to protect the innocence of children.

"They've been captured," Darden explained. "They took them to the jailhouse. We have to help them!"

"I don't understand. Why would they put innocent children in jail? What did you kids do to get into trouble?"

"Nothing!" Darden replied. "It's Alystra. They wanted Alystra! Now they're all in trouble."

"Oh, my!" Matilda exclaimed. "That little boy... now I see it... It was Princess Alystra the whole time! In my house! Goodness me!"

Forthright	(**fawrth**-rahyt) – ADJ – frank; going straight to the point
Incandescent	(in-kuhn-**des**-uhnt) – ADJ – glowing with heat; brilliant
Predispose	(pree-di-**spohz**) – V – to give a tendency beforehand; to render liable
Stricture	(**strik**-cher) – N – a critical remark; a restriction

"We've got to help them!"

The old woman gave him a knowing nod. She now realized the grave danger the prisoners were in. There was a long pause before she was able to speak, as Matilda tried to determine what to do.

"Belaynee clearly has plans to destroy the supporters of the Administrator. They put out a decree." The woman *cited* the banners hung about the town, "All Traitors Be Hanged!" as evidence of her claim. She said, "They will surely charge that Alystra and your friends are insurgents."

"Oh, no!" Darden exclaimed.

"I'll bet the jailhouse is *fraught* with soldiers and officers, probably more crowded than a bustling anthill. With that much protection, I don't know how we're supposed to even think about helping them escape."

"We have to do something!" Darden cried. "We have to save my brother!"

Matilda paused a moment, then immediately went to her desk. She opened a drawer and began rustling through various items. Matilda revealed herself to be an *antiquary* as she carefully shifted around a large number of old and rare items while searching. She then pulled out a round metallic badge attached to a string. She placed it around her neck, and wore it like a *periapt* to ward off evil.

"What's that?"

"This is my Officer of Ministry shield. I got this as an Army Pilot. It used to allow me access to many sites and places in regard to religious affairs. I don't know if it'll work to get inside the jailhouse, but it's worth a shot."

Cite	(sahyt) – V – to quote; to recall
Fraught	(frawt) – ADJ – filled or laden
Antiquary	(**an**-ti-kwair-ee) – N – an expert or collector of antiquities
Periapt	(**per**-ee-apt) – N – an amulet or magical charm

"OK! Let's go!"

"Hold on, dear one." She responded. "They're not going to be accepting religious visits in the middle of the night. We'll have to wait it out until the morning. Then we'd have reason to go. Your brother and friends will be fine tonight. Belaynee's not going to let anything happen unless he's there to oversee it... and I can promise you, he's a late sleeper. Now, let me find my *ecclesiastical* robes, so I can at least look the part."

Although waiting was *adverse* to everything inside telling him to help his brother as quickly as possible, Darden relented. They needed a plan of attack, and being rash wouldn't help anybody. Patience was the plan, but it was hard for him to swallow.

Darden didn't sleep that night. Rescuing his brother was his *capital* concern, much more important than getting rest. He sat in a chair and thought, and because thinking wasn't his strong suit, the best thought he could come up with was *Elihu will have a plan. He'll know what to do. I just have to talk to him.*

In the morning, Matilda found him still sitting where she had left him. He hadn't moved an inch.

"Are you OK, honey?"

"I'm fine. I'm just scared."

"Listen, son. I'm a minister of religion, or at least I used to be one. It's my right to see those children, and as long as there's a good *pious* person in control, they will not deny

Ecclesiastical	(ih-klee-zee-**as**-ti-kuhl) – ADJ – churchly; not secular
Adverse	(ad-**vurs**) – ADJ – opposite or opposing in purpose or effect
Capital	(**kap**-i-tl) – ADJ – principal; highly important; first-rate
Pious	(**pahy**-uhs) – ADJ – having or showing reverence for god; sanctimonious

me for sake of conscience. We can figure it out from there."

"Elihu," Darden responded. "Elihu will know what to do. You talk to the guards, let me sneak in to talk to Elihu. He lives for this sort of thing, always reading about strategies and what not. He's a genius, some kind of *savant*, you know."

"For some reason, I think somehow that might work... but it doesn't make a lick of sense. I've got a feeling your brother has the answer, and my instincts never get it wrong."

"Let's bring some rope too," Darden said. "Elihu's plans almost always include rope." Darden smiled as they began to get ready for their mission. The two rescuers' timely arrival at the jailhouse was *concurrent* to the mass exodus of soldiers. The few remaining big trucks were filled with passengers and then shipped off. Dust flew in the air as the vehicles roared away, and almost instantly the jail became deserted.

"There's a window around back," Matilda explained. "It looks like we're in luck. The soldiers have all left. I'll go to the front and talk with the guards. You sneak around and see if you can catch sight of your friends."

The boy nodded his head and took off around back. Matilda placed her silver ministry badge on her chest and straightened her ecclesiastical robes—her appearance was completely passable. She walked to the front, and rang the bell. Gene answered in his typical cowboy demeanor.

"What do you want?" he demanded.

"I'm here to speak to your prisoners. I have been called to tend to their spiritual needs."

Savant	(sa-**vahnt**) – N – a person of profound learning; a scholar
Concurrent	(kuhn-**kur**-uhnt) – ADJ – occurring at the same time; cooperating

"No can do, sister. No visitors."

"They're just children; please behave in a *civil* manner. After all, religious conference is part of citizen privilege."

Darden used this time to make a *seamless* transition to the back of the jailhouse with the rope. He dashed behind rocks and obstacles, and was able to make it around back without alerting Gene. A barred window to the cell was a little higher than Darden was tall. He grabbed a box, set it next to the wall, and climbed up to peek inside. The three children were all huddled together, moping. That is until Darden whistled softly.

Elihu immediately recognized the sound of his brother. His eyes lit up, and he rushed over to the window. He was filled with nothing but raving *plaudits* for his brother.

"Darden! You wonderful, exceptional brother!" he exclaimed. "How did you do it? Where did you come from? Where have you been? I always knew you were smart and clever and capable of coming through!"

"Matilda helped me. She's distracting the guard so we can talk," Darden responded.

"We don't have much time!" Elihu exclaimed. "You have to get us out immediately. What's the plan?"

"I don't know. I was hoping that you would have one. After all, we've always relied on your great mischievous prowess to help us make plans and escape the worst situations."

Civil	(**siv**-uhl) – ADJ – pertaining to citizenship; marked by benevolence
Seamless	(**seem**-lis) – ADJ – having no seams; smoothly continuous
Plaudit	(**plaw**-dit) – N – an enthusiastic expression of approval

"Well," Elihu began. "It just so happens I do have a plan. Listen here..."

Meanwhile, Gene and Matilda continued to **banter** lightly back and forth. Clearly, neither of them wanted to give in, so they continued to try to one-up each other with their remarks. That is, until Darden came walking up to the front door, whistling. Gene immediately lost interest in Matilda and latched onto the boy.

"What do you think you're doing!" he exclaimed. "How did you get out here?"

"Teleport," Darden gave his **specious** response with wide-eyed innocence. "I told ya I would... and I'll do it again if you put me back."

"You worthless, dumb, horrible..." Gene **decried**, until noticing Matilda's shocked face. "I mean, foolish young boy. Will you ever learn?"

He gave the priestly woman a false smile, as he pretended to be nice to the helpless boy.

"I am thankful that you don't use such **ribaldry** around the impressionable children. It's easy for men of your type to get a reputation for indecent speech and **bawdy** language, but I'm glad to see you respect their innocence."

"Yes, ma'am," he responded. "Nothing but the best for my prisoners."

Gene ushered Darden into the prison house and turned to the middle-aged woman.

Banter	(**ban**-ter) – N – an exchange or playful remarks
Specious	(**spee**-shuhs) – ADJ – plausible but not genuine
Decry	(dih-**krahy**) – V – to condemn; to denounce
Ribaldry	(**rib**-uhl-dree) – N – vulgar or indecent character or speech
Bawdy	(**baw**-dee) – ADJ – indecent; lewd

"Now, if you'll excuse me." He shut the door in her face.

The gruff man dragged Darden to the cell where the rest of the *subjugated* children were waiting submissively. However, now only Maleck and Alystra were visible.

"I don't know why you came back here, kid," Gene said as he began unlocking the door. "I don't get it. They always come back."

Gene chuckled as he recalled all the many drunks and pranksters who returned to the slammer day after day. The *recidivism* rate in Prairieton was astounding; the average citizen had multiple jail stays every month.

Dragging Darden inside the cell into the corner where Maleck and Alystra stood together, the guard attempted to *aggregate* his prisoners into the same place. He hovered over them.

"Don't you dare try a stunt like that again! I'll be watching you so closely that you won't even be able to breathe without me noticing!"

Unfortunately for Gene, he had walked right into the trap that the children had set for him. Elihu leaped into action. Hiding on the top bunk, he was equipped with a blanket and rope. He jumped on the man and covered him with the blanket. Gene fell to the ground and the other kids pounced as well, until the man was thoroughly subdued and tied up.

Maleck grabbed the jailer's keys and led the others outside the cell. He locked the gate.

"Later! I won't miss you!"

Subjugate	(**suhb**-juh-geyt) – V – to make submissive; to bring under control
Recidivism	(ri-**sid**-uh-viz-uhm) – N – repeated or habitual relapse, as in crime
Aggregate	(**ag**-ri-geyt) – V – to bring together; collect into one sum

The four kids rushed outside to find Matilda waiting for them with her cruiser. Elihu grabbed his brother by the shoulder with great pride.

"I always knew you had an inborn **aptitude** for invention! You saved us all!"

Darden responded with a smile. "I guess after all these years you've been a pretty good affluence on me."

Although Elihu immediately recognized the **malapropism**, he didn't come right out and tell Darden he had used the wrong word. He didn't want to ruin his brother's moment in the sun, although he did try a subtle correction, which went unnoticed.

"Yeah, I guess I have been a pretty good *influence* after all."

Although the entire group was happy and excited to have escaped the jailhouse, the **preponderant** emotion was that of urgency. Alystra rushed over to Matilda and gave her a great big hug, and couldn't contain herself.

"We have to go to the Cherkle Den! That's where they're taking my father. We have to do something!"

"I don't know what we can do," Matilda responded gravely. "It's us versus the whole army. Maybe we need to look for more help?"

"No!" Elihu responded. "Belaynee and his men are wickedly **conniving** right now to kill the Administrator. Time is of the essence!"

Aptitude	(**ap**-ti-tood) – N – capability; quickness in learning
Malapropism	(**mal**-uh-prop-iz-uhm) – N – the act of misusing words ridiculously
Preponderant	(pri-**pon**-der-uhnt) – ADJ – superior in weight or influence
Connive	(kuh-**nahyv**) – V – to conspire; to pretend ignorance of or fail to act against wrongdoing

"We have to go now!" Alystra exclaimed. "They could throw him in any minute!"

"Maybe they'll just hold him there and threaten him or something. You know, wait for a little while?" Darden added hopefully, trying to reassure her.

Elihu had little hope for any sort of *moratorium* to delay the Administrator's inevitable execution. Belaynee was going to do the deed as quickly as possible. They needed a plan, one that allowed immediate action and still provided a call for help. Somehow they needed to find a *synthesis* of the two parts. That's when it came to him.

"Didn't they say that Belaynee's warship was there?" Elihu asked.

"Yeah," responded Maleck. "That's not encouraging at all."

"The warship is our answer. That's how we'll save the Administrator."

"Son, a warship is gigantic and full of weapons and soldiers, and almost impossible to destroy in battle," Matilda said.

"We'll blow it up from the inside!" Elihu exclaimed.

"What are you talking about?" Maleck asked.

"Every warship for the last 130 years has been built with a self-destruct mechanism, just in case it ever got into the wrong hands. It's part of Allied regulations."

"You're kidding, right?" Maleck asked, concerned.

"No, listen! We can find Alystra's father, get him out, and then make Belaynee's ship self-destruct. It's perfect! Any time a major ship explodes, the Peacekeeping

Moratorium	(mawr-uh-**tawr**-ee-uhm) – N – a suspension of activity; a period of waiting
Synthesis	(**sin**-thuh-sis) – N – the combining of the constituent elements of separate material

Commission automatically sends help. If we don't escape, we'll be rescued for sure!"

"I don't like it," Maleck declared. "Seems too risky. Do you even know how to turn on a self-destruct mechanism?"

"Darden can figure out any computer system," Elihu said confidently.

Matilda opened her vehicle and motioned for the kids to get in. The kids began to pile in, but Maleck paused. This was going to be dangerous, but he knew they had to put an end to Belaynee's vile actions and *sordid* intentions. He realized that they had little time to come up with an alternative plan, so he relented.

"OK. Let's do it!"

Sordid   (**sawr**-did) – ADJ – morally ignoble; vile; meanly self-seeking

WORD REVIEW

Abrogate	Connive	Preponderant
Adverse	Decry	Recidivism
Aggregate	Ecclesiastical	Ribaldry
Antiquary	Forthright	Savant
Aptitude	Fraught	Seamless
Banter	Incandescent	Sordid
Bawdy	Malapropism	Specious
Bereft	Moratorium	Stricture
Capital	Periapt	Subjugate
Cite	Pious	Synthesis
Civil	Plaudit	
Concurrent	Predispose	

9

The *pneumatic* sounds of high velocity winds beat against the vehicle as they drove through the high desert. The reunited foursome sat together in the back, mentally preparing for their coming adventure. Much like every other aspect of this crazy journey, they had no idea how they were going to pull off their plan. Maleck looked sick to his stomach while Darden and Elihu were both pensive. Alystra kept her eyes closed in silent *supplication,* praying for the safety of her friends, and even more so, her father.

Their small vehicle finally reached the outskirts of the Cherkle Den, which was a gaping hole in the center of the earth. Although the travelers were still very far away, they could hear the sounds of the cherkles underground echo through the desert basin. This only served as an *affirmation* of their fears that today's journey would be very dangerous.

Belaynee's warship hovered beside the great gorge. It was a military vehicle so large that it could hold thousands of men. Like a huge floating bunkhouse, it remained in the air surrounded by all the parked military ships in the dirt below it.

Pneumatic	(noo-**mat**-ik) – ADJ – pertaining to air, gases or wind
Supplicate	(**suhp**-li-keyt) – V – to pray humbly; make a earnest petition
Affirmation	(af-er-**mey**-shuhn) – N – confirmation of the truth

On the ground was a wooden stage, built from the *boughs* of immense trees. The large wooden planks were placed perpendicular to the pit, so that all the wood grain pointed directly toward the ledge. One of the greatest planks of wood was made from a large tree trunk. It extended beyond the cavern and over the Cherkle Den, for "Walking the plank." Soldiers stood at *concentric* positions around the hole and were able to watch the happening from every vantage point of the circle. Perhaps this was to prove a point: This is what happens if you go rogue.

The rescuers had decided on the elements of their plan. Matilda would dock at the warship, pretending to have a package. She would stall the soldiers at the gate, not being able to find her delivery, while the kids would slip out of the loading bay. Darden and Elihu, who refined the craft of hacking ship computer systems at Earlmont, would use this knowledge to hack into the computer and set the ship to self-destruct. Meanwhile Maleck and Alystra would go down to the platform and create a distraction to *contravene* the ceremony until the ship exploded. Then help would arrive.

Without any fanfare, Matilda brought her cruiser to the loading bay of the huge ship. She was given permission to park and a ship guard approached her. As she got out, the four children *bilked* their potential captors by taking a secretive exit out the other side.

Maleck grabbed Darden and Elihu by the shoulders before letting them depart.

"Good luck, guys. Be safe." He said quietly.

Bough	(bou) – N – a large tree branch
Concentric	(kuhn-**sen**-trik) – ADJ – having a common center
Contravene	(kon-truh-**veen**) – V – to deny or oppose; to violate
Bilk	(bilk) – V – to defraud; to frustrate; to escape

They nodded.

"If anything happens, I want you to know that you two are my best friends."

"We agree," Elihu responded, noting the *parity* of emotion. "Remember, once you see Matilda's vehicle leave the loading bay you have ten minutes before the ship explodes. We don't want to lose you."

This interchange was an absolute revelation for Maleck. All his life he had been looking for friends like these, and now he had finally found them. Although their relationship was still in an *embryonic* stage, it was clear that if given the opportunity to mature, they would be the best of friends for life. It's funny how the most frightening of circumstances can somehow bring out the best in people.

Maleck looked toward Alystra, and she motioned for them to get moving. They took off toward the Cherkle Den. The twins began to sneak their way inside the interior of the ship.

On the other side of the bay, the guard followed Matilda to the back of her vehicle. On the back latch was a key code to open the trunk containers. She began putting in numbers, but immediately messed up.

"I'm sorry," she said. "So clumsy."

She messed it up again, and then again. She seemed unable to open the back. She pretended to be *chagrined* with embarrassment by the whole situation.

"I don't know what's wrong. I just locked this up this morning."

Parity	(**par**-i-tee) – N – having equality; equivalence
Embryonic	(em-bree-**on**-ik) – ADJ – rudimentary; undeveloped
Chagrin	(shuh-**grin**) – N – a feeling of vexation marked by humiliation

"What's going on here, lady?" the guard remarked suspiciously.

"Oh, nothing! I'll get it done this time!"

Remarkably, Matilda was immediately able to open the door with ease. She gave the man a weak smile.

"See, I knew I could do it."

She began looking through the contents of the hatch. "They *consigned* a really important package to me to deliver… Now where did I put it?"

The man stepped closer to her, his raised eyebrows *evincing* a growing disbelief in Matilda's story. She felt his suspicious eyes, and turned away.

"OK, I guess it's not here."

Matilda looked at her shipping list, "Look here! I was supposed to go to the other big ship in Prairieton."

She showed the man her shipping list, and although it had no such listing, she moved it away from his face so fast he was unable to notice the discrepancy.

"Gotta go! Later!"

"Hold it here, lady!" the man exclaimed. "What's going on? You're hiding something."

Matilda took a moment, and then nodded her head. She looked at the guard, ready to confess.

"I'm sorry. I just wanted to help these kids, but I realize now that it's only going to cause more problems in the long run."

"What kids?"

"The orphans of Prairieton. They're having a fundraiser right now to build a new school room. I thought maybe if I could sneak onto this ship, I could talk to

Consign	(kuhn-**sahyn**) – V – to hand over; to set apart
Evince	(ih-**vins**) – V – to prove; to show clearly

Roman... He's such a great leader, you know... If I could talk to him and tell him about the children, he would do something... I'm sorry, it was stupid."

"Listen here, lady," the guard replied. "Stunts like this could get you into some major trouble. But I see you didn't mean any harm. Let me talk to my supervisor. Maybe we can do something about these orphans, but right now I need you to get off my ship. You don't have clearance."

"OK. Thank you so much. I'm sorry for any inconvenience."

Matilda got back into her vehicle, started the engine, and began to leave.

* * *

In the loading bay Darden and Elihu sneaked behind crates and boxes piled to be transported into the ship until finally they reached the main entrance where a horde of soldiers paced back and forth. All this time, they hadn't spoken one word. As twins, they had shared an *innate* sense of communication without words for as long as they could remember. Hand signals, motions of the head, and even things as small as eye movement conveyed countless thoughts between them. Now they had reached a point where actual language was necessary. They needed to figure out how to *ford* a passage through the river of army men.

"What are we going to do? How are we supposed to get in there?" Darden asked.

Innate	(ih-**neyt**) – ADJ – inborn; inherent in the essential character of something
Ford	(fohrd) – V – to cross a river at a low point

"I don't know, but we need to access the main computer system... and there seems to be a limitless number of *entrenched* soldiers blocking our way."

Darden tapped his brother on the shoulder. On the opposite wall, partially hidden behind a stack of boxes, was the universal *ideogram* depicting a computer system.

"Darden! You're a genius!"

Elihu hugged his brother and the two went over to the wall with the symbol. A large metal plate covered the main connection, so they began to pry at it. Darden took off his shoe and began to bang on it, until Elihu noticed the control frame button. He pressed it, and the computer console opened up.

"We make a good team, I think," Elihu said, happy about their joint discovery.

Darden took the helm and began typing. There were millions of lines of code and information. The system seemed almost alien in design and construction, but he was not fazed. Compared to hacking into Earlmont's heavily fortified system, this would be simple. The ship was running on a 30-year-old operating system. It should be easy for him to find unguarded entry points. He knew he had to succeed even if it got complicated. The destruction of this ship was the deciding *linchpin* in the success of their mission. Even if Maleck and Alystra could rescue the Administrator, there was no way they could escape without the arrival of the Peacekeeping Commission.

Entrenched	(en-**trench**-d) – ADJ – established firmly; in a position of security
Ideogram	(**id**-ee-uh-gram) – N – a symbol, rather than a word, that represents an idea
Linchpin	(**linch**-pin) – N – a pin that holds everything together

* * *

Maleck and Alystra found a space elevator on the ship's exterior and took it down to the ground below. They reached the outskirts of the platform just as Roman Belaynee was about to *inaugurate* the ceremonial process of putting the Administrator to death. Alystra's father was bound by the hands, and beat up a little in the face, but otherwise unharmed. Belaynee paced back and forth in front of him, sizing him up. He pulled a *fob* from his coat and checked the time on the attached clock.

"Well, sir," he said. "It's about that time. Do you have anything you want to say for yourself? Confess to treason, perhaps?"

The Administrator snarled at his adversary. "You're the traitor, Roman! You're no better than a filthy animal!"

Belaynee shushed the prisoner with a wave of his hand.

"Moderately aggressive for one's last speech, I'm afraid," Belaynee continued. "I did think you would at least have some sense of civil *propriety*. It's customary to say something meaningful or quotable for your last speech, but I guess you'll just have to go to your death looking like a coward."

"You'll be known for illegally *ousting* the proper ruler! The history books will look down on you as a power-hungry glutton!"

Inaugurate	(in-**aw**-gyuh-reyt) – V – to commence with a formal ceremony
Fob	(fob) – N – a small chain attached to an ornament; a pocket watch
Propriety	(pruh-**prahy**-i-tee) – N – conformance to standards; appropriateness to circumstances
Oust	(oust) – V – to remove from place occupied

"Perhaps," Belaynee replied. "But that will be years after I live a long, productive life... Now walk the plank!"

The crowd of soldiers began to shout as they pushed the Administrator forward. Slowly, step by step, he moved up the large wooden plank toward the opening of the Cherkle Den. The sounds of growling and gnashing teeth bellowed from deep inside. As he neared, he watched the sand from the sides flow into the deep abyss like *molten* lava pouring from a volcano. For the first time in his captivity, he was scared. Suddenly shouts came from the other side.

"Stop! Stop! Let go of him!" a girlish voice called out.

The execution ceremony was abruptly *adjourned*, as the crowd of soldiers directed their attention toward the voice. The Administrator walked backward toward the platform, recognizing his daughter's voice. In the distance, he could see the apparition of a little girl accompanied by a dark-haired boy. Belaynee turned to the children.

"Well, well," he said. "If it isn't Little Miss Princess, come to save her daddy... I'll admit, I'm impressed. I don't know how you got here, or out of jail for that matter, but I guess love conquers all, right?"

"We don't want to fight you," she said in a *conciliatory* manner. "We just want my father safe."

"Oh," he said, sounding surprised. "Is that all you want? OK. No big deal... GET THEM!" he screamed.

Soldiers surrounded the two children and apprehended them. Their arms were tied together, and they were pushed toward the plank with the Administrator.

Molten	(**mohl**-tn) – ADJ – melted; liquefied by heat
Adjourn	(uh-**jurn**) – V – to suspend or postpone to a later time
Conciliatory	(kuhn-**sil**-ee-uh-tawr-ee) – ADJ – tending to overcome hostility

"Why are you doing this?" she pleaded. "We can't hurt you!"

"It has nothing to do with you. This is my legacy. Silva is my territory now, and I can't have any resistance rallying around the daughter of the former Administrator. Getting rid of you is key to securing my reign."

"You're an egotistical monster!" she exclaimed, marveling at the man's extreme *megalomania*. She couldn't believe he would kill innocent children just to make himself great.

"I won't abide such *irreverence* from a child! Don't you dare backtalk me… I'll make sure you watch your father walk the plank first."

Belaynee motioned for them to be forced to the plank where the Administrator remained. The kids joined the regal-looking man on the plank. He shook his head regretfully.

"I'm so sorry, honey," her dad said. "I'm going to get you out of this. Don't worry." The man looked at Belaynee in agony. "Please! Let them go. They will never cause you any harm. I will do anything! Anything! Just let my daughter go!"

The evil antagonist did nothing but let out a loud and *robust* laugh.

"That's the funniest thing I have ever heard!" He continued to laugh, as Maleck looked anxiously toward the ship. If only the twins would blow it up already, then they could escape. *What is taking them so long? What if they got caught? What if it all ends here?*

Megalomania	(meg-uh-loh-**mey**-nee-uh) – N – an obsession with doing grand things
Irreverence	(ih-**rev**-er-uhns) – N – lack of respect
Robust	(roh-**buhst**) – ADJ – strong and healthy; boisterous

"Enough!" Belyanee shouted. "Start walking!"

The guard held weapons directly toward the three on the plank. They had no choice but to walk. The Administrator took position first, followed by Maleck, and then Alystra.

The scene became *funereal* as the three began their march to certain death. Slowly, step by step, they moved, getting closer and closer to the vile sounds of the evil monsters. The Administrator walked all the way to the end and turned around.

"Alystra, sweetie," he said sadly. "I'm sorry about this. If I could do it all over again, I would find a way to keep you safe until the end. I love you, baby."

Maleck looked back at the ship. *Come on! Blow up! Hurry!* But nothing happened.

As the Administrator slowly turned around, reluctant to make the plunge, there was a long *pregnant* pause. Then, a siren sound blasted through the crowd of guards. Suddenly, Matilda's cruiser approached the center of the ring. She appeared, gun in hand, with a hard face and *martial* attire, ready for war.

"Let them go, or I'll shoot!"

All eyes went to the hefty woman who was wearing a metallic breastplate and a feather headdress. Although hundreds of guns were pointed at the people on the plank, nobody was around to protect Belaynee from a clear shot from the woman. The guns repositioned themselves to face Matilda.

"If you shoot me, I'll shoot him! I'll take him with

Funereal	(fyoo-**neer**-ee-uhl) – ADJ – gloomy or mournful; fitting a funeral
Pregnant	(**preg**-nuhnt) – ADJ – full of meaning; abounding or filled
Martial	(**mahr**-shuhl) – ADJ – warlike; characteristic of a warrior

me," she declared ***adamantly***.

"Hold your fire!" Belaynee called. "This crazy, fat, insane woman thinks she can stop me? You should know, woman, I can do whatever I want. I'm in charge now."

Not wanting to be the sole object of ***derision*** and laughter, Matilda smarted back. "Well, you're a mean, ugly enemy!"

Before anyone had a chance to do anything more, the sound of an explosion ripped through the sky. All eyes moved toward the large ship. A ***fissure*** tore down the main hull, ripping it in half. Billows of smoke rose from the ship, with flames ensuing. The self-destruct mechanism had detonated in the engine room, but the fire would soon overtake the warship. Darden and Elihu hoped that this slight delay would give the soldiers enough time to escape without any harm.

The scene became chaotic instantly. Soldiers began running toward the ship as the sky turned red. In the distance, the three prisoners rushed off the plank. In the confusion, nobody was watching anything. The next thing Belaynee realized, a gun barrel was at his neck, and crazy Matilda stood there, eyes locked on him.

"You'd best start walking." She shoved the gun at him and he began to walk.

"Ha ha," he responded. "This is kind of a funny turn of events. When I said crazy and fat, you do realize I was joking, right?"

She pushed the gun farther, and he stumbled down the plank.

"I can do whatever I want. I'm in charge now," she

Adamant	(**ad**-uh-muhnt) – ADJ – unyielding; hard to break
Derision	(dih-**rizh**-uhn) – N – ridicule; mockery
Fissure	(**fish**-er) – N – a narrow opening produced by cleavage or separation

exclaimed.

"Oh," he responded. "That's funny because I just said that, huh? Aren't you clever?" He tried to laugh, but her face remained angry. "Well, you don't have to be so hardhearted about it. It was mainly a joke in the first place."

She pushed him farther down the plank to the very edge. Belaynee was a *doctrinaire* of his evil anarchy and hadn't thought about the consequences to him if it failed.

"Jump." She commanded.

After a moment of hesitation, Roman Belaynee looked around to find that all his men had deserted him. The monsters began to growl furiously beneath his shaky perch. He looked down and saw the horrific movement of the creatures below. In a flash, Belayanee turned around and began to run toward Matilda, but his legs got caught up together and he tripped, falling into the darkness, screaming the whole way down.

Matilda returned to the platform, where Maleck, Alystra, and the Administrator stood stunned. They watched as she holstered her gun.

"What?" she exclaimed. "It had to be done… Now don't just stand there. We've got to get out of this place!"

She opened the cruiser doors and the former prisoners hopped inside. Matilda took off as fast as she could, heading directly for the self-destructing ship. The once hovering vehicle had now crashed into the ground. They watched as the outer shell and *infrastructure* tore into pieces. Sides were falling off, windows were breaking,

Doctrinaire	(dok-truh-**nair**) – N – a person who applies a doctrine without practical considerations
Infrastructure	(in-fruh-**struhk**-cher) – N – the underlying framework of a system

and all manner of debris fell in pieces.

Black smoke filled the air; out of the *detritus* appeared two small, pale boys with blue and green eyes. They were covered in black, but all smiles. Matilda stopped her vehicle amid the commotion and opened the door.

"Come on!" she yelled.

They hopped in, and the van made an egress away from the horrific scene.

"Everything went according to plan, even the escape. Once the self-destruct sirens started blaring, nobody watched as we grabbed a hover Reken and took off," Elihu explained.

"You guys did it!" Maleck exclaimed. "You saved us!"

"I guess our efforts were rather *effectual*," Elihu responded humbly.

Darden then realized a *palpable* sense of somebody watching him. He looked to his left, and saw Alystra sitting right beside him.

"Hi," he said, half-embarrassed to be so close.

"You saved me," she responded. "Again."

Before Darden had a chance to think or react or do anything, Alystra kissed him on the cheek. *What a day!*

The group flew off to safety.

Detritus	(dih-**trahy**-tuhs) – N – debris; small particles broken away
Effectual	(ih-**fek**-choo-uhl) – ADJ – valid; producing the intended effect
Palpable	(**pal**-puh-buhl) – ADJ – easily perceived; capable of being touched

WORD REVIEW

Adamant	Effectual	Linchpin
Adjourn	Embryonic	Martial
Affirmation	Entrenched	Megalomania
Bilk	Evince	Molten
Bough	Fissure	Oust
Chagrin	Fob	Palpable
Concentric	Ford	Parity
Conciliatory	Funereal	Pneumatic
Consign	Ideogram	Pregnant
Contravene	Inaugurate	Propriety
Derision	Infrastructure	Robust
Detritus	Innate	Supplicate
Doctrinaire	Irreverence	

10

Debilitating apprehension was all that Maleck could feel as their ship moved closer and closer to Acritas and his expected punishment. His legs felt numb and his heart weak. He had swallowed so much spit that his mouth had become severely dry.

When the Peacekeeping Commission arrived on Planet Silva, it was decided that Maleck would return home instead of to Earlmont Academy. Due to his knavish antics, he had been expelled...again. One cannot play such pranks and escape the ship without getting into some form of trouble.

Facing his parents was not the worst part, for he had faced Azreel and Beol Vise Plutean many times before. It was worse now because all his new friends would be there to see him get in trouble. The Peacekeeping Commission had sent only one ship to rescue them, so Alystra, the twins, and the Administrator were all on board with him, and Acritas was the first stop.

Maleck knew a report had been sent to his parents chronicling his most recent adventure. Commandeering Earlmont's video center, stealing an evac pod, going to jail, blowing up a large ship, overthrowing a planet's

---

Debilitate   (dih-**bil**-i-teyt) – V – to make weak or feeble

government *et al.*—never had Maleck gotten into so much mischief. The Vise Pluteans had a knack for creating humiliating and embarrassing punishments. Once they made him paint the house in his underwear on a Saturday so all the other kids could watch him. Another time he was spanked on the stage in the school auditorium during a school-wide conference. Whatever their punishment, it would set the *benchmark* for most horrifying and scary, cruel and unusual. They would be waiting for him as he arrived, and ready to dole it out.

Maleck tried to keep his mind on other things. He liked to pretend that maybe their ship was headed to some warm, tropical hideaway where he could swim through the coral of the beautiful *atoll* in crystal clear water. Maybe they could make a quick pit stop on the way, so he and his friends could have a chance to enjoy each other's company before imminent doom.

It was no use pretending. On the horizon, Maleck could see the *fawn* planet creep closer, like a sphere of dirty yellow sand. *Yuck! This is an ugly, crowded place to be. Not wild and empty like Silva.*

He watched as the lights from all the buildings and factories came into view. Although he would never consider himself a *pundit* with qualification to comment, Maleck thought there would have to be a million places better than Acritas. This place was cold, filthy, and crowded. He

Et Al.	(et **al**) – N – and others; and elsewhere
Benchmark	(**bench**-mahrk) – N – a standard of excellence or achievement
Atoll	(**at**-awl) – N – a ring-shaped coral reef
Fawn	(fawn) – ADJ – light yellowish-brown
Pundit	(**puhn**-dit) – N – an expert; a person who makes comments or judgments

wanted to go back to where it was warm, wild, and empty. Acritas had no *husbandry* to sustain its natural resources. If he were in charge, he would do things different. He would change stuff. That's when Maleck realized he was just like his parents.

Ever since moving to this planet, Maleck had had a bad attitude. His parents were given the opportunity to serve on the High Council, but they never considered Maleck's opinion in the matter. He knew they wanted to help make Acritas a better place, but Maleck's negative feelings about the place had always *nullified* their intentions in his mind. Finally he realized that maybe his feelings were not as important as his parents choice to do the right thing. He also realized the good his parents had already done and how they had already made positive changes. For instance, the Acritas school system had declined to a sorry state of *atrophy* when they arrived. One of their first priorities was to reallocate funds to improve facilities and increase grade standards significantly. Maleck always thought that this was intended to make his life harder, but now he saw that it was really for the good of everyone, regardless of his feelings.

They also advocated a *retrenchment* to the overly generous entertainment subsidies provided by the government. Although they wholeheartedly supported the arts, they did not think it wise for personal video devices to

Husbandry	(**huhz**-buhn-dree) – N – careful or thrifty management; farming
Nullify	(**nuhl**-uh-fahy) – V – to declare void; to make ineffective
Atrophy	(**a**-truh-fee) – N – degeneration or decrease from disuse
Retrenchment	(ri-**trench**-muhnt) – N – cutting down by reduction of expenses

be bought with tax money for each individual's enjoyment. This was another horrific decision that finally started to make sense to the young lad. *Maybe his parents were more than just **bureaucrats** unenthusiastically involved in government, but rather real change-makers.*

As the Peacekeeping Commission ship began its descent into Acritas, Maleck was unable to stop the *incessant* thoughts of the punishment his parents would mete out. The dark-haired boy prepared himself in the exit chamber. His friends entered as well, excited to meet Maleck's family and to see his hometown.

"We finally get to meet your folks!" Darden exclaimed. "Aren't you excited?"

"Yeah, I guess," Maleck responded weakly.

"There's nothing to worry about," the Administrator added with sincere *probity*. "They will be glad to see that you're safe."

"They're going to be very angry. Just to warn everybody, they're really nice people and you'll like them when they calm down, but forgive them if their speech is filled with biting *acrimony*."

"Not to mean any *diminution* or disregard of your fears," Elihu countered, "but I'm sure it won't be that bad."

At that point, the ship landed.

Bureaucrat	(**byoor**-uh-krat) – N – an official of a bureaucracy, esp. one who follows routine in an unimaginative way
Incessant	(in-**ses**-uhnt) – ADJ – unending; without interruption
Probity	(**proh**-bi-tee) – N – integrity; honesty
Acrimony	(**ak**-ruh-moh-nee) – N – bitterness or harshness
Diminution	(dim-uh-**noo**-shuhn) – N – the process of diminishing

"We're here," Alystra said, as the door to the ship began to open to the great bustling platform of Acritas.

Maleck immediately noticed his father Azreel standing solemnly outside, waiting for him. He wore his formal council robes, the ones he wore during criminal trials, complete with the blue shoulder *epaulet* that signified ceremonial occasions.

Almost trembling, Maleck approached his father. His friends walked behind him, allowing a safe distance between them and the wrath of Azreel.

"Hello, Father," Maleck said timidly.

"Maleck Vise Plutean, for what purpose did you leave school and find yourself here today?" he asked sternly.

In beginning his story, Maleck *broached* the subject honestly, realizing that his father was probably already familiar with the truth.

"Well..." he started. "I was up to no good as usual, and I did a prank, and before I got in trouble, I kind of lifted an evac pod and crash-landed on a planet, where some bad stuff was happening, and I tried to help out, but we did destroy a battleship and call the Peacekeeping Commission—"

"I'm very proud of you," Azreel interrupted.

Maleck's eyes grew wide. This pleasant response was very *divergent* from the anger he was expecting.

"The Peacekeeping Commission filled us in on the whole scenario. The insurgency on Planet Silva has been a point of concern for the entire quadrant. For months we

---

Epaulet	(**ep**-uh-let) – N – an ornamental shoulder piece esp. military
Broach	(brohch) – V – to suggest for the first time; to tap
Divergent	(dih-**vur**-juhnt) – ADJ – differing; deviating

have been trying to bring about a peaceful *rapprochement* with the new regime to no avail. We were in the process of trying to figure out how to solve the problem, when it suddenly got resolved by four children."

"This is a joke, right?" Maleck asked.

"Your actions were silly, irresponsible, and foolhardy," Azreel continued. "But also very brave and admirable."

"Really?"

"Yes, and as such, you and all your friends have been recommended for membership in the Bronze Medallion, the most distinguished society for humanitarian aid and scientific exploration in the galaxy, supporting *anthropocentric* causes universally."

"Ha ha!" blurted out Elihu. "Take that Xayx! You're not so special after all!"

Azreel continued. "Although I do not approve of your previous behavior and the causes that led up to your heroic deeds, I consider them *extrinsic* to this current honor."

"What does that mean?" Maleck questioned. His father smiled and dropped his formal tone.

"It means you're still getting punished for them."

"Oh."

"But on a brighter note, the Bronze Medallion also comes with a yearly *stipend*… money to be used to further good throughout the galaxy. It's quite a large sum."

Rapprochement	(rap-rohsh-**mahn**) – N – an establishment of harmonious relations
Anthropocentric	(an-thruh-poh-**sen**-trik) – ADJ – regarding the human being as the central fact of the universe
Extrinsic	(ik-**strin**-sik) – ADJ – not essential; being external
Stipend	(**stahy**-pend) – N – periodic payment, esp. a scholarship

"Cool," Maleck responded.

"I'm really proud of you, son. You left for Earlmont as a rough aluminum *ingot* needing to be shaped and refined, and you returned a Bronze Medallion."

Azreel reached out his arms and gave his son a loving embrace. Finally, Maleck was home once again. His father pulled back with a smile.

"I can't believe you went to Planet Exile! My very own son! You're a real gunslinger now, huh? You know, your mother would never let me visit there. 'Too many riffraffs,' she says."

"Yeah, I guess it was pretty cool," Maleck responded. "The land of adventure and danger, they say."

Azreel noticed the group of people standing behind Maleck, patiently waiting for the father and son reunion to conclude.

"Now, let me meet your friends!" he exclaimed.

Maleck gladly introduced his father to his new best friends, Elihu and Darden, and then, of course, to the Administrator and his daughter. Azreel welcomed the group to Acritas and congratulated them on all their successes.

* * *

By the end of the week, Maleck's parents were able to decide on a punishment. It seemed only appropriate that he be forced to *expurgate* the city walls of graffiti using a small polisher to undo years of defacement.. Fortunately for him, his new friends were allowed to help him in the

---

Ingot	(**ing**-guht) – N – a mass of metal convenient for shaping
Expurgate	(**ek**-sper-geyt) – V – to cleanse of moral offensiveness

process. Although truthfully, none of the other three children were much help.

Alystra arrived wearing a ***gossamer*** gown made of expensive Treilsive silk, which she refused to get dirty. The twins, too, were so busy arguing that they provided little aid to the endeavor.

"Everyone else agrees that the money should go to some charity, for furtherance of good," Elihu stated.

"But I want to buy a spaceship!" Darden said. "We could go exploring and help mankind by discovering unknown territories and worlds!" Ever since Darden had been forced to find independence while Elihu was imprisoned, the idea of making his own decisions intoxicated him. He could no longer be agreeably ***pliant***, and thus found it necessary to contradict Elihu as much as possible.

"You're just being a belligerent ***polemic***!" Elihu exclaimed. "You don't always have to disagree with everything!"

Maleck couldn't help but laugh on the inside at their conversation. It was awesome and strange to him that even though they looked identical, although not always divergent, their personalities were completely ***disparate***. Each definitely had his own way of thinking.

"What do you think, Maleck?" Elihu commanded.

Gossamer	(**gos**-uh-mer) – N – something extremely delicate; any light fabric
Pliant	(**plahy**-uh nt) – ADJ – easy to bend or influence; compliant
Polemic	(puh-**lem**-ik) – N – a controversial argument; a person who argues controversies
Disparate	(**dis**-per-it) – ADJ – distinct in kind; essentially different

"Shouldn't we give the money to charitable causes? I know I'm not alone in thinking that."

Although their adventures on Planet Silva had nearly gotten them killed several times, and Maleck was supremely tired of all the aimless wanderings, his sense of adventure was still *extant*.

"I don't know," he replied. "I think it could be fun to buy a small ship, and go explore."

"WHAT?!?" Elihu exclaimed. "That contrary response is what I get for *presupposing* you had any decent amount of logical reasoning skills! Clearly, you don't."

"Presupposing someone would agree with you isn't using very good logical reasoning skills either," *scintillated* Alystra playfully.

She walked over to her new crush, Darden, and latched onto his arm. "I agree with Darden. Let's go sailing!"

"This is a silly *deciduous* whim! It will be short-lived, once some sense gets knocked into you all," Elihu proclaimed. "Mark my words, you will all change your mind when you realize how much a spaceship costs and how hard it would be on board for an extended period of time... and when you realize that we're not going to be allowed to go anywhere without the supervision of an adult!"

Elihu was quite proud of his logic. More than any of the other children, he definitely had a way of seeing all the outcomes and establishing a clear depiction of reality. Truthfully, Elihu liked the idea of spontaneous action.

Extant	(ek-**stuhnt**) – ADJ – in existence; not destroyed
Presuppose	(**pree**-suh-pohz) – V – to suppose or assume beforehand
Scintillate	(**sin**-tl-yet) – V – to emit sparks; to sparkle with wit
Deciduous	(dih-**sij**-oo-uhs) – ADJ – not permanent; transitory like leaves

He just didn't like that he hadn't come up with the idea himself.

"So, I'm right!" he concluded.

The other children looked at the ground quietly. Almost immediately, Elihu's mind was harshly *lacerated* with the idea that something was going on behind his back.

"What's going on here?"

"What if..." Darden ventured. "We already found a ship?"

"And found a skilled, *reputable* captain to sail with us?" Maleck added.

"In three days?" Elihu became angered, "If you think I'm willing to partake in some intergalactic *maritime* adventure on the high celestial seas without even being considered..."

"And," interrupted Alystra, "we already decided to make you First Mate—second in charge only to the captain!"

"Well..."

"Not to mention," added Darden, "the best sailing team since the *heyday* of the Femozy Armada, the high point of space exploration. That's us, your best friends!"

Elihu sighed. His friends knew him all too well. His two favorite things, being in charge and being with his friends, made the offer almost irresistible. It was somehow able to reawaken a *dormant* desire for adventure, which

---

Lacerate	(**las**-uh-reyt) – V – to tear roughly; to distress mentally
Reputable	(**rep**-yuh-tuh-buhl) – ADJ – held in good repute; honorable
Maritime	(**mar**-i-tahym) – ADJ – pertaining to the sea; nautical
Heyday	(**hey**-dey) – N – period of greatest vigor or strength
Dormant	(**dawr**-muhnt) – ADJ – inactive; asleep

Elihu's logical side had been trying to put to sleep.

"OK," he declared, "that may be acceptable... You didn't really get a ship did you?"

Within seconds, a loud, whirring noise came from above. An apparition of a small spacecraft drifted down toward the children, and soon became very clearly *corporeal.* The door opened wide, and who should appear but Matilda, dressed like a medieval *Cossack* wearing a brown turban, fur-lined boots, and leather sportscoat.

"Who's ready for adventure!" she exclaimed.

Elihu looked at his friends and smiled.

"We all are," he responded.

The kids picked up their *sundry* marble polishing supplies and loaded them onto the vehicle. Maleck was the last to get in, and was proud to find his newfound friends all together and ready to fly off on another exciting *odyssey.* This was the start of something spectacular.

Corporeal	(kawr-**pawr**-ee-uhl) – ADJ – of the physical body; tangible or material
Cossack	(**kos**-ak) – N – a horseman from Russia
Sundry	(**suhn**-dree) – ADJ – various or diverse
Odyssey	(**od**-uh-see) – N – a traveling adventure

WORD REVIEW

Acrimony
Anthropocentric
Atoll
Atrophy
Benchmark
Broach
Bureaucrat
Corporeal
Cossack
Debilitate
Deciduous
Diminution
Disparate
Divergent

Dormant
Epaulet
Et Al.
Expurgate
Extant
Extrinsic
Fawn
Gossamer
Heyday
Husbandry
Incessant
Ingot
Lacerate
Maritime

Nullify
Odyssey
Pliant
Polemic
Presuppose
Probity
Pundit
Rapprochement
Reputable
Retrenchment
Scintillate
Stipend
Sundry

GLOSSARY

Abdicate - (**ab**-di-keyt) - V - to renounce or relinquish the right - page 58 - chapter 5

Abhor - (ab-**hawr**) - V - to regard with extreme disgust; detest - page 48 - chapter 4

Abomination - (uh-bom-uh-**ney**-shuhn) - N - a vile, shameful action or condition - page 61 - chapter 5

Abrogate - (**ab**-ruh-geyt) - V - to abolish; to put an end to - page 91 - chapter 8

Accentuate - (ak-**sen**-choo-yet) - V - to make more noticable; to emphasize - page 85 - chapter 7

Accrue - (uh-**kroo**) - V - to grow or add to in time - page 19 - chapter 2

Acrimony - (**ak**-ruh-moh-nee) - N - bitterness or harshness - page 120 - chapter 10

Adamant - (**ad**-uh-muhnt) - ADJ - unyielding; hard to break - page 113 - chapter 9

Adduce - (uh-**doos**) - V - to bring forward in argument or as evidence - page 75 - chapter 6

Adherent - (ad-**heer**-uhnt) - N - a person who supports a cause; a follower - page 51 - chapter 4

Adjourn - (uh-**jurn**) - V - to suspend or postpone to a later time - page 110 - chapter 9

Adverse - (ad-**vurs**) - ADJ - opposite or opposing in purpose or effect - page 94 - chapter 8

Aesthetic - (es-**thet**-ik) - ADJ - pertaining to a sense of beauty - page 48 - chapter 4

Affable - (**af**-uh-buhl) - ADJ - friendly; easy to approach; pleasant - page 22 - chapter 2

Affirmation - (af-er-**mey**-shuhn) - N - confirmation of the truth - page 103 - chapter 9

Aggregate - (**ag**-ri-geyt) - V - to bring together; collect into one sum - page 98 - chapter 8

Ague - (**ey**-gyoo) - N - a fit of fever, shivering, or chills - page 75 - chapter 6

Allegiance - (uh-**lee**-juhns) - N - loyalty to a person or group - page 58 - chapter 5

Altercation - (awl-ter-**key**-shuhn) - N - a heated or angry dispute - page 29 - chapter 2

Amass - (uh-**mas**) - V - to collect; to come together - page 33 - chapter 3

Anarchy - (**an**-er-kee) - N - a society without government or law - page 68 - chapter 6

Anomie - (**an**-uh-mee) - N - the breakdown of social norms and values - page 70 - chapter 6

Anterior - (an-**teer**-ee-er) - ADJ - placed in the front; coming before - page 82 - chapter 7

Anthropocentric - (an-thruh-poh-**sen**-trik) - ADJ - regarding the human being as the central fact of the universe - page 122 - chapter 10

Antiquary - (**an**-ti-kwair-ee) - ADJ - an expert or collector of antiquities - page 93 - chapter 8

Aplomb - (uh-**plom**) - N - (1)vertical position; (2)having poise - page 11 - chapter 1

Appurtenance - (uh-**pur**-tn-uhns) - N - something subordinate to a more important thing - page 39 - chapter 3

Aptitude - (**ap**-ti-tood) - N - capability; quickness in learning - page 99 - chapter 8

Articulate - (ahr-**tik**-yuh-lit) - ADJ - uttered clearly; having clarity and effectiveness - page 28 - chapter 2

Atavistic - (at-uh-**vis**-tik) - ADJ - reverting to an earlier type; throwback - page 23 - chapter 2

Atoll - (**at**-awl) - N - a ring-shaped coral reef - page 118 - chapter 10

Atrophy - (**a**-truh-fee) - N - degeneration or decrease from disuse - page 119 - chapter 10

August - (aw-**guhst**) - ADJ - venerable; eminent - page 70 -
chapter 6

Austere - (aw-**steer**) - ADJ - severe in appearance;
without ornament; serious - page 19 - chapter 2

Autocratic - (aw-tuh-**krat**-ik) - ADJ - tyrannical; domineering -
page 24 - chapter 2

Avuncular - (uh-**vuhng**-kyuh-ler) - ADJ - characteristic of an
uncle - page 87 - chapter 7

Balk - (bawk) - V - to stop and refuse to proceed - page 40 -
chapter 3

Bamboozle - (bam-**boo**-zuhl) - V - to deceive; to perplex -
page 23 - chapter 2

Banter - (**ban**-ter) - N - an exchange or playful remarks -
page 97 - chapter 8

Bawdy - (**baw**-dee) - ADJ - indecent; lewd - page 97 -
chapter 8

Beget - (bih-**get**) - V - to cause; produce as an effect -
page 82 - chapter 7

Belie - (bih-**lahy**) - V - to show to be false; to misrepresent -
page 15 - chapter 1

Benchmark - (**bench**-mahrk) - N - a standard of excellence
or achievement - page 118 - chapter 10

Bequeath - (bih-**kweeth**) - V - to hand down; pass on -
page 57 - chapter 5

Bereft - (bih-**reft**) - ADJ - deprived - page 91 -
chapter 8

Bilk - (bilk) - V - to defraud; to frustrate; to escape -
page 104 - chapter 9

Blowhard - (**bloh**-hahrd) - N - a boastful and talkative
person - page 34 - chapter 3

Bluster - (**bluhs**-ter) - V - to be loud, noisy; to roar, as wind -
page 52 - chapter 4

Bombast - (**bom**-bast) - N - pompous speech; pretentious
words - page 42 - chapter 3

Bona Fide - (**boh**-nuh fahyd) - ADJ - made in good faith; authentic - page 57 - chapter 5

Bough - (bou) - N - a large tree branch - page 104 - chapter 9

Braggart - (**brag**-ert) - N - a person who brags a lot - page 70 - chapter 6

Brawn - (brawn) - N - muscular strength - page 22 - chapter 2

Brazen - (**brey**-zuhn) - ADJ - shameless or impudent; like brass - page 14 - chapter 1

Broach - (brohch) - V - to suggest for the first time; to tap - page 121 - chapter 10

Bureaucrat - (**byoor**-uh-krat) - N - an official of a bureaucracy, esp. one who follows routine in an unimaginative way - page 120 - chapter 10

Burnish - (**bur**-nish) - V - to polish; make smooth - page 81 - chapter 7

Calamity - (kuh-**lam**-i-tee) - N - a great misfortune; affliction - page 39 - chapter 3

Calloused - (**kal**-uhs) - ADJ - hardened; insensitive - page 62 - chapter 5

Capital - (**kap**-i-tl) - ADJ - principal; highly important; firstrate - page 94 - chapter 8

Capricious - (kuh-**pree**-shuhs) - ADJ - indicative of whim; erratic - page 41 - chapter 3

Carapace - (**kar**-uh-peys) - N - a bony shell; shield - page 84 - chapter 7

Careworn - (**kair**-wohrn) - ADJ - showing signs of care or worry - page 62 - chapter 5

Censorious - (sen-**sohr**-ee-uhs) - ADJ - severely critical; fault-finding - page 71 - chapter 6

Chagrin - (shuh-**grin**) - N - a feeling of vexation marked by humiliation - page 105 - chapter 9

Charisma - (kuh-**riz**-muh) - N - special ability of leadership or popularity - page 58 - chapter 5

Charlatan - (**shahr**-luh-tn) - N - a person who deceives by
appearance - page 16 - chapter 1

Chide - (chahyd) - V - to express disapproval; to nag -
page 30 - chapter 2

Chortle - (**chawr**-tl) - V - to chuckle gleefully - page 34 -
chapter 3

Chronicle - (**kron**-i-kuhl) - V - to record as in a chronicle -
page 56 - chapter 5

Circuitous - (ser-**kyoo**-i-tuhs) - ADJ - roundabout; not direct -
page 48 - chapter 4

Cite - (sahyt) - V - to quote; to recall - page 93 -
chapter 8

Civil - (**siv**-uhl) - ADJ - pertaining to citizenship; marked
by benevolence - page 96 - chapter 8

Cloister - (**kloi**-ster) - N - a quiet, secluded place, esp.
religious - page 41 - chapter 3

Cloy - (kloi) - V - to weary by an excess of food or pleasure;
to satiate - page 60 - chapter 5

Complacent - (kuhm-**pley**-suhnt) - ADJ - pleased
and unaware of danger - page 82 -
chapter 7

Concentric - (kuhn-**sen**-trik) - ADJ - having a common
center - page 104 - chapter 9

Conciliatory - (kuhn-**sil**-ee-uh-tawr-ee) - ADJ - tending to
overcome hostility - page 110 - chapter 9

Concurrent - (kuhn-**kur**-uhnt) - ADJ - occurring at the same
time; cooperating - page 95 - chapter 8

Congenital - (kuhn-**jen**-i-tl) - ADJ - existing from birth;
inherent - page 76 - chapter 6

Connive - (kuh-**nahyv**) - V - to conspire; to pretend
ignorance of or fail to act against wrongdoing -
page 99 - chapter 8

Consign - (kuhn-**sahyn**) - V - to hand over; to set apart -
page 106 - chapter 9

Construe - (kuhn-**stroo**) - V - analyze and explain a phrase, especially in connection with translating - page 83 - chapter 7

Contravene - (kon-truh-**veen**) - V - to deny or oppose; to violate - page 104 - chapter 9

Corkage - (**kawr**-kij) - N - a fee charged for serving wine in a restaurant - page 87 - chapter 7

Corporeal - (kawr-**pawr**-ee-uhl) - ADJ - of the physical body; tangible or material - page 127 - chapter 10

Corpulent - (**kawr**-pyuh-luhnt) - ADJ - fat; portly - page 72 - chapter 6

Cossack - (**kos**-ak) - N - a horseman from Russia - page 127 - chapter 10

Cower - (**kou**-er) - V - to crouch, as in fear - page 78 - chapter 6

Crass - (kras) - ADJ - without refinement; gross - page 60 - chapter 5

Credo - (**kree**-doh) - N - any creed or formula of belief - page 84 - chapter 7

Crony - (**kroh**-nee) - N - a close friend; chum - page 13 - chapter 1

Dapple - (**dap**-uhl) - N - a spot or mottled marking - page 81 - chapter 7

De Facto - (dee **fak**-toh) - N - in fact; in reality - page 51 - chapter 4

Debilitate - (dih-**bil**-i-teyt) - V - to make weak or feeble - page 117 - chapter 10

Decadent - (**dek**-uh-duhnt) - ADJ - characterized by cultural or moral depravity - page 67 - chapter 6

Deciduous - (dih-**sij**-oo-uhs) - ADJ - not permanent; transitory like leaves - page 125 - chapter 10

Decry - (dih-**krahy**) - ADJ - to condemn; to denounce - page 97 - chapter 8

Defile - (dih-**fahyl**) - V - to make impure or dirty - page 13 - chapter 1

Delinquent - (dih-**ling**-kwuhnt) - ADJ - neglectful of a duty; overdue - page 68 - chapter 6

Demagogue - (**dem**-uh-gog) - N - a person who gains power by arousing emotions - page 58 - chapter 5

Demerit - (dih-**mer**-it) - N - a mark of misconduct; fault - page 20 - chapter 2

Depose - (dih-**pohz**) - V - to remove from office; to affirm under oath - page 57 - chapter 5

Derision - (dih-**rizh**-uhn) - N - ridicule; mockery - page 113 - chapter 9

Detritus - (dih-**trahy**-tuhs) - N - debris; small particles broken away - page 115 - chapter 9

Diminution - (dim-uh-**noo**-shuhn) - N - the process of diminishing - page 120 - chapter 10

Disaffect - (dis-uh-**fekt**) - V - to alienate the affections - page 11 - chapter 1

Disclaim - (dis-**kleym**) - V - to disown connection with; to deny - page 37 - chapter 3

Disconcert - (dis-kuhn-**surt**) - V - to perturb; to disarrange - page 63 - chapter 5

Disparate - (**dis**-per-it) - ADJ - distinct in kind; essentially different - page 124 - chapter 10

Dissent - (dih-**sent**) - V - to disagree; to differ in opinion - page 42 - chapter 3

Dissolution - (dis-uh-**loo**-shuhn) - N - the undoing or breaking into parts - page 71 - chapter 6

Divergent - (dih-**vur**-juhnt) - ADJ - differing; deviating - page 121 - chapter 10

Doctrinaire - (dok-truh-**nair**) - N - a person who applies a doctrine without practical considerations - page 114 - chapter 9

Dormant - (**dawr**-muhnt) - ADJ - inactive; asleep - page 126 - chapter 10

Dross - (dros) - N - waste matter; refuse - page 45 - chapter 4

Dupe - (doop) - N - a person who is easily fooled - page 24 - chapter 2

Dyspeptic - (dis-**pep**-tik) - ADJ - gloomy or pessimistic; pertaining to dyspepsia - page 40 - chapter 3

Ecclesiastical - (ih-klee-zee-**as**-ti-kuhl) - ADJ - churchly; not secular - page 94 - chapter 8

Eddy - (**ed**-ee) - N - a small whirlpool; a trend counter to the main current - page 46 - chapter 4

Effectual - (ih-**fek**-choo-uhl) - ADJ - valid; producing the intended effect - page 115 - chapter 9

Effusive - (ih-**fyoo**-siv) - ADJ - unduly demonstrative; lacking reserve - page 59 - chapter 5

Egress - (**ee**-gres) - N - exit; the right to go out - page 59 - chapter 5

Eloquent - (**el**-uh-kwuhnt) - ADJ - having or exercising the power of fluent, forceful, and appropriate speech - page 63 - chapter 5

Embroil - (em-**broil**) - V - to throw into confusion; to bring discord - page 34 - chapter 3

Embryonic - (em-bree-**on**-ik) - ADJ - rudimentary; undeveloped - page 105 - chapter 9

En Masse - (en **mas**) - N - all together; as a group - page 40 - chapter 3

Encumbrance - (en-**kuhm**-bruhns) - N - something burdensome; hindrance - page 76 - chapter 6

Enmity - (**en**-mi-tee) - N - a feeling of hostility - page 16 - chapter 1

Entrenched - (en-**trench**-d) - ADJ - established firmly; in a position of security - page 108 - chapter 9

Epaulet - (**ep**-uh-let) - N - an ornamental shoulder piece esp. military - page 121 - chapter 10

Equanimity - (ek-wuh-**nim**-i-tee) - N - calmness; equilibrium - page 30 - chapter 2

Ermine - (**ur**-min) - N - white fur, esp. to identify royalty or high rank - page 60 - chapter 5

Esplanade - (**es**-pluh-nahd) - N - any open, level space, especially for a public walk or drive - page 69 - chapter 6

Et Al. - (et **al**) - N - and others; and elsewhere - page 118 - chapter 10

Evince - (ih-**vins**) - V - to prove; to show clearly - page 106 - chapter 9

Exhort - (ig-**zawrt**) - V - to urge; advise; caution - page 72 - chapter 6

Exigency - (**ek**-si-juhn-see) - N - urgency; situation needing prompt action - page 21 - chapter 2

Expatriate - (eks-**pey**-tree-yet) - V - to banish (a person) from his country - page 17 - chapter 1

Expurgate - (**ek**-sper-geyt) - V - to cleanse of moral offensiveness - page 123 - chapter 10

Extant - (ek-**stuhnt**) - ADJ - in existence; not destroyed - page 125 - chapter 10

Extrinsic - (ik-**strin**-sik) - ADJ - not essential; being external - page 122 - chapter 10

Façade - (fuh-**sahd**) - N - superficial appearance of something - page 21 - chapter 2

Fanaticism - (fuh-**nat**-uh-sahyz-uhm) - N - fanatical character and spirit - page 70 - chapter 6

Fawn - (fawn) - ADJ - light yellowish-brown - page 118 - chapter 10

Ferrous - (**fer**-uhs) - ADJ - containing iron - page 45 - chapter 4

Fickle - (**fik**-uhl) - ADJ - likely to change, esp. due to caprice - page 87 - chapter 7

Fiefdom - (**feef**-duhm) - N - domain of a feudal lord - page 36 - chapter 3

Fissure - (**fish**-er) - N - a narrow opening produced by cleavage or separation - page 113 - chapter 9

Fob - (fob) - N - a small chain attached to an ornament; a pocket watch - page 109 - chapter 9

Foolhardy - (**fool**-hahr-dee) - ADJ - recklessly bold; foolishly rash - page 17 - chapter 1

Ford - (fohrd) - V - to cross a river at a low point - page 107 - chapter 9

Forthright - (**fawrth**-rahyt) - ADJ - frank; going straight to the point - page 92 - chapter 8

Fraternal - (fruh-**tur**-nl) - ADJ - brotherly; befitting brothers - page 88 - chapter 7

Fraught - (frawt) - ADJ - filled or laden - page 93 - chapter 8

Funereal - (fyoo-**neer**-ee-uhl) - ADJ - gloomy or mournful; fitting a funeral - page 112 - chapter 9

Futile - (**fyoot**-ul) - ADJ - frivolous; ineffective - page 50 - chapter 4

Gamesome - (**geym**-suhm) - ADJ - playful; frolicsome - page 23 - chapter 2

Gamin - (**gam**-in) - N - street urchin - page 14 - chapter 1

Garrulous - (**gar**-uh-luhs) - ADJ - excessively talkative; wordy - page 46 - chapter 4

Genesis - (**jen**-uh-sis) - N - an origin or beginning - page 50 - chapter 4

Gerrymander - (**jer**-i-man-der) - V - dividing voting districts to favor a certain party - page 57 - chapter 5

Gild - (gild) - V - to give a bright or pleasing aspect to something - page 19 - chapter 2

Glacial - (**gley**-shuhl) - ADJ - bitterly cold; moving slowly - page 11 - chapter 1

Gossamer - (**gos**-uh-mer) - N - something extremely delicate; any light fabric - page 124 - chapter 10

Grandiose - (**gran**-dee-ohs) - ADJ - affectedly important; pompous - page 36 - chapter 3

Gregarious - (gri-**gair**-ee-uhs) - ADJ - fond of others; sociable - page 84 - chapter 7

Gridiron - (**grid**-ahy-ern) - N - any framework or network resembling a gridiron - page 20 - chapter 2

Guise - (gahyz) - N - general external appearance; assumed appearance - page 35 - chapter 3

Hale - (heyl) - ADJ - free from disease; vigorous - page 49 - chapter 4

Heyday - (**hey**-dey) - N - period of greatest vigor or strength - page 126 - chapter 10

Hirsute - (hur-**soot**) - ADJ - hairy; shaggy - page 52 - chapter 4

Hoarfrost - (**hawr**-frawst) - N - frost; a covering of minute ice needles - page 51 - chapter 4

Husbandry - (**huhz**-buhn-dree) - N - careful or thrifty management; farming - page 119 - chapter 10

Iconoclast - (ahy-**kon**-uh-klast) - N - a person who attacks cherished beliefs - page 14 - chapter 1

Ideogram - (**id**-ee-uh-gram) - N - a symbol, rather than a word, that represents an idea - page 108 - chapter 9

Impecunious - (im-pi-**kyoo**-nee-uhs) - ADJ - having little or no money; poor - page 34 - chapter 3

Imperceptive - (im-per-**sep**-tiv) - ADJ - lacking perception - page 36 - chapter 3

Impetuous - (im-**pech**-oo-uhs) - ADJ - moving with great force; a sudden, rash action - page 83 - chapter 7

Imponderable - (im-**pon**-der-uh-buhl) - ADJ - not ponderable; cannot be determined - page 16 - chapter 1

Impromptu - (im-**promp**-too) - ADJ - made without previous preparation; improvised - page 75 - chapter 6

Inaugurate - (in-**aw**-gyuh-reyt) - V - to commence with a
formal ceremony - page 109 - chapter 9

Incandescent - (in-kuhn-**des**-uhnt) - ADJ - glowing with heat;
brilliant - page 92 - chapter 8

Incessant - (in-**ses**-uhnt) - ADJ - unending; without inter-
ruption - page 120 - chapter 10

Inclination - (in-kluh-**ney**-shuhn) - N - a preference; state of
being inclined - page 74 - chapter 6

Inculcate - (in-**kuhl**-keyt) - V - to implant by repeated
statement; teach persistently - page 17 - chapter 1

Indigent - (**in**-di-juhnt) - ADJ - poor; impoverished -
page 87 - chapter 7

Inert - (in-**urt**) - ADJ - inactive or sluggish - page 71 -
chapter 6

Infamy - (**in**-fuh-mee) - N - extremely bad reputation -
page 19 - chapter 2

Infinitesimal - (in-fin-i-**tes**-uh-muhl) - ADJ - infinitely small;
minute - page 50 - chapter 4

Infrastructure - (in-fruh-**struhk**-cher) - N - the underlying
framework of a system - page 114 - chapter 9

Ingot - (**ing**-guht) - N - a mass of metal convenient for
shaping - page 123 - chapter 10

Innate - (ih-**neyt**) - ADJ - inborn; inherent in the essential
character of something - page 107 - chapter 9

Instigate - (**in**-sti-geyt) - V - to urge or provoke - page 41 -
chapter 3

Insuperable - (in-**soo**-per-uh-buhl) - ADJ - incapable of
being beaten - page 52 - chapter 4

Interlope - (**in**-ter-lohp) - V - to intrude without approval -
page 12 - chapter 1

Interpolate - (in-**tur**-puh-leyt) - V - to introduce between two
things - page 36 - chapter 3

Inveigle - (in-**vey**-guhl) - V - to ensnare by flattery - page 30 -
chapter 2

Irreverence - (ih-**rev**-er-uhns) - N - lack of respect - page 111 - chapter 9

Itinerant - (ahy-**tin**-er-uhnt) - ADJ - traveling from place to place - page 76 - chapter 6

Jubilation - (joo-buh-**ley**-shuhn) - N - a feeling of festive celebration - page 76 - chapter 6

Junoesque - (joo-noh-**esk**) - ADJ - stately or regal (as a woman) - page 16 - chapter 1

Knavish - (**ney**-vish) - ADJ - untrustworthy; dishonest - page 17 - chapter 1

Lacerate - (**las**-uh-reyt) - V - to tear roughly; to distress mentally - page 126 - chapter 10

Larder - (**lahr**-der) - N - pantry or supply of food - page 56 - chapter 5

Laxity - (**lak**-si-tee) - N - state of being loose or lenient - page 83 - chapter 7

Libertarian - (lib-er-**tair**-ee-uhn) - ADJ - advocating liberty or free will - page 56 - chapter 5

Linchpin - (**linch**-pin) - N - a pin that holds everything together - page 108 - chapter 9

Listless - (**list**-lis) - ADJ - having little interest; spiritless - page 77 - chapter 6

Loiter - (loi-ter) - V - to linger aimlessly; to move in a slow manner - page 74 - chapter 6

Lucre - (**loo**-ker) - N - monetary reward or gain - page 61 - chapter 5

Malapropism - (**mal**-uh-prop-iz-uhm) - N - the act of misusing words ridiculously - page 99 - chapter 8

Manifest - (**man**-uh-fest) - ADJ - obvious; apparent - page 38 - chapter 3

Maritime - (**mar**-i-tahym) - ADJ - pertaining to the sea; nautical - page 126 - chapter 10

Marshal - (**mahr**-shuhl) - N - military officer; sheriff - page 86 - chapter 7

Martial - (**mahr**-shuhl) - ADJ - warlike; characteristic of a
warrior - page 112 - chapter 9

Megalomania - (meg-uh-loh-**mey**-nee-uh) - N - an obsession
with doing grand things - page 111 - chapter 9

Mercantile - (**mur**-kuhn-teel) - ADJ - of or pertaining to
merchants; engaged in trade - page 77 -
chapter 6

Mettle - (**met**-l) - N - courage and fortitude; temperament -
page 37 - chapter 3

Mnemonic - (ni-**mon**-ik) - ADJ - assisting memory;
pertaining to mnemonics or memory - page 30 -
chapter 2

Molten - (**mohl**-tn) - ADJ - melted; liquefied by heat - page 110 -
chapter 9

Moratorium - (mawr-uh-**tawr**-ee-uhm) - N - a suspension of
activity; a period of waiting - page 100 - chapter 8

Munificent - (myoo-**nif**-uh-suhnt) - ADJ - very generous -
page 56 - chapter 5

Muster - (**muhs**-ter) - V - to gather together; to assemble
for battle - page 55 - chapter 5

Myopia - (mahy-**oh**-pee-uh) - N - lack of foresight; narrow-
mindedness - page 42 - chapter 3

Nemesis - (**nem**-uh-sis) - N - something that cannot be
conquered; a rival - page 53 - chapter 4

Nonchalant - (non-shuh-**lahnt**) - ADJ - coolly unconcerned
or indifferent; casual - page 27 - chapter 2

Notoriety - (noh-tuh-**rahy**-i-tee) - N - state of being known
widely, esp. unfavorably - page 13 - chapter 1

Nullify - (**nuhl**-uh-fahy) - V - to declare void; to make
ineffective - page 119 - chapter 10

Obsequious - (uhb-**see**-kwee-uhs) - ADJ - showing servile
deference; obedient - page 71 - chapter 6

Odyssey - (**od**-uh-see) - N - a traveling adventure - page 127 -
chapter 10

Ordinance - (**awr**-dn-uhns) - N - a command; a public
    regulation - page 36 - chapter 3
Oust - (oust) - V - to remove from place occupied -
    page 110 - chapter 9
Oxymoron - (ok-si-**mawr**-on) - N - a figure of speech that
    seems self-contradictory - page 85 - chapter 7
Paean - (**pee**-uhn) - N - any song of praise or joy - page 15 -
    chapter 1
Palpable - (**pal**-puh-buhl) - ADJ - easily perceived; capable
    of being touched - page 115 - chapter 9
Paragon - (**par**-uh-gon) - N - model of excellence - page 12 -
    chapter 1
Parity - (**par**-i-tee) - N - having equality; equivalence -
    page 105 - chapter 9
Patrician - (puh-**trish**-uhn) - ADJ - aristocratic; like a
    person of high rank - page 61 - chapter 5
Peckish - (**pek**-ish) - ADJ - rather irritable; somewhat
    hungry - page 47 - chapter 4
Periapt - (**per**-ee-apt) - N - an amulet or magical charm -
    page 93 - chapter 8
Pervade - (per-**veyd**) - V - to spread throughout all parts -
    page 37 - chapter 3
Petulant - (**pech**-uh-luhnt) - ADJ - showing impatient
    irritation - page 29 - chapter 2
Phoenix - (**fee**-niks) - N - a person or thing of beauty;
    paragon - page 67 - chapter 6
Pious - (**pahy**-uhs) - ADJ - having or showing reverence for
    god; sanctimonious - page 94 - chapter 8
Plaudit - (**plaw**-dit) - N - an enthusiastic expression of
    approval - page 96 - chapter 8
Plebiscite - (**pleb**-uh-sahyt) - N - a vote to decide an
    important decision - page 47 - chapter 4
Pliant - (**plahy**-uh nt) - ADJ - easy to bend or influence;
    compliant - page 124 - chapter 10

Pneumatic - (noo-**mat**-ik) - ADJ - pertaining to air, gases or wind - page 103 - chapter 9

Polemic - (puh-**lem**-ik) - N - a controversial argument; a person who argues controversies - page 124 - chapter 10

Populous - (**pop**-yuh-luhs) - ADJ - crowded; full of residents - page 28 - chapter 2

Precipitous - (pri-**sip**-i-tuhs) - ADJ - extremely steep; characterized by precipices - page 45 - chapter 4

Predicament - (pri-**dik**-uh-muhnt) - N - an unpleasantly difficult situation - page 38 - chapter 3

Predispose - (pree-di-**spohz**) - V - to give a tendency beforehand; to render liable - page 92 - chapter 8

Pregnant - (**preg**-nuhnt) - ADJ - full of meaning; abounding or filled - page 112 - chapter 9

Premonition - (pree-muh-**nish**-uhn) - N - a forewarning; anticipating a future event - page 73 - chapter 6

Preponderant - (pri-**pon**-der-uhnt) - ADJ - superior in weight or influence - page 99 - chapter 8

Presuppose - (**pree**-suh-pohz) - V - to suppose or assume beforehand - page 125 - chapter 10

Privation - (prahy-**vey**-shuhn) - N - lack of the usual comforts; act of depriving - page 49 - chapter 4

Probity - (**proh**-bi-tee) - N - integrity; honesty - page 120 - chapter 10

Prodigious - (pruh-**dij**-uhs) - ADJ - extraordinary in size; wonderful or marvelous - page 28 - chapter 2

Prognosticate - (prog-**nos**-ti-keyt) - V - to predict; to prophesy - page 27 - chapter 2

Promontory - (**prom**-uhn-tawr-ee) - N - a bluff or plateau; a high point of land in the sea - page 48 - chapter 4

Propriety - (pruh-**prahy**-i-tee) - N - conformance to standards; appropriateness to circumstances - page 109 - chapter 9

Prudent - (**prood**-nt) - ADJ - wise or judicious in practical affairs; careful in planning - page 25 - chapter 2

Pundit - (**puhn**-dit) - N - an expert; a person who makes comments or judgments - page 118 - chapter 10

Querulous - (**kwer**-uh-luhs) - ADJ - full of complaints - page 29 - chapter 2

Queue - (kyoo) - N - a file for waiting in line; a braid of hair - page 25 - chapter 2

Rapprochement - (rap-rohsh-**mahn**) - N - an establishment of harmonious relations - page 122 - chapter 10

Rarefied - (**rair**-uh-fahyd) - ADJ - highly elevated; belonging to a select group - page 22 - chapter 2

Recidivism - (ri-**sid**-uh-viz-uhm) - N - repeated or habitual relapse, as in crime - page 98 - chapter 8

Regime - (ruh-**zheem**) - N - system of government; government in power - page 68 - chapter 6

Reprobate - (**rep**-ruh-beyt) - ADJ - morally depraved; unprincipled - page 74 - chapter 6

Reputable - (**rep**-yuh-tuh-buhl) - ADJ - held in good repute; honorable - page 126 - chapter 10

Retrenchment - (ri-**trench**-muhnt) - N - cutting down by reduction of expenses - page 119 - chapter 10

Ribaldry - (**rib**-uhl-dree) - N - vulgar or indecent character or speech - page 97 - chapter 8

Robust - (roh-**buhst**) - ADJ - strong and healthy; boisterous - page 111 - chapter 9

Sallow - (**sal**-oh) - ADJ - of a sickly or yellowish color - page 37 - chapter 3

Sanguine - (**sang**-gwin) - ADJ - cheerful and confident; optimistic - page 24 - chapter 2

Savant - (sa-**vahnt**) - N - a person of profound learning; a scholar - page 95 - chapter 8

Scintillate - (**sin**-tl-yet) - V - to emit sparks; to sparkle with wit - page 125 - chapter 10

Seamless - (**seem**-lis) - ADJ - having no seams; smoothly continuous - page 96 - chapter 8

Sedulous - (**sej**-uh-luhs) - ADJ - diligent in attention; assiduous - page 87 - chapter 7

Silo - (**sahy**-loh) - N - a structure that stores food or missiles - page 53 - chapter 4

Sinecure - (**sahy**-ni-kyoor) - N - an office or position requiring little or no work - page 27 - chapter 2

Slovenly - (**sluhv**-uhn-lee) - ADJ - untidy or unclean in appearance; slipshod - page 62 - chapter 5

Solidarity - (sol-i-**dar**-i-tee) - N - community of purpose; having unity - page 41 - chapter 3

Sordid - (**sawr**-did) - ADJ - morally ignoble; vile; meanly self-seeking - page 101 - chapter 8

Spate - (speyt) - N - a sudden outpouring - page 24 - chapter 2

Specious - (**spee**-shuhs) - ADJ - plausible but not genuine - page 97 - chapter 8

Spurious - (**spyoor**-ee-uhs) - ADJ - not genuine or authentic; counterfeit - page 25 - chapter 2

Squadron - (**skwod**-ruhn) - N - persons grouped together for a similar purpose - page 21 - chapter 2

Stalactite - (stuh-**lak**-tahyt) - N - a deposit hanging from the roof of a cave - page 64 - chapter 5

Static - (**stat**-ik) - ADJ - fixed in a stationary condition; showing little or no change - page 49 - chapter 4

Stentorian - (sten-**tawr**-ee-uhn) - ADJ - very loud or powerful in sound - page 33 - chapter 3

Stipend - (stahy-pend) - N - periodic payment, esp. a scholarship - page 122 - chapter 10

Stricture - (**strik**-cher) - N - a critical remark; a restriction - page 92 - chapter 8

Subjugate - (**suhb**-juh-geyt) - V - to make submissive; to bring under control - page 98 - chapter 8

Suffrage - (**suhf**-rij) - N - the right to vote; a vote given - page 47 - chapter 4

Sundry - (**suhn**-dree) - ADJ - various or diverse - page 127 - chapter 10

Supplicate - (**suhp**-li-keyt) - V - to pray humbly; make a earnest petition - page 103 - chapter 9

Surly - (**sur**-lee) - ADJ - churlishly rude; unfriendly or hostile - page 33 - chapter 3

Swagger - (**swag**-er) - V - to walk or strut; to boast noisily - page 26 - chapter 2

Synthesis - (**sin**-thuh-sis) - N - the combining of the constituent elements of separate material - page 100 - chapter 8

Temerity - (tuh-**mer**-i-tee) - N - reckless boldness; rashness - page 46 - chapter 4

Utopian - (yoo-**toh**-pee-uhn) - ADJ - resembling utopia; involving idealized perfection - page 26 - chapter 2